GARDEN SASS:
A Catalog of Arkansas Folkways

GARDEN SASS:

A Catalog of
Arkansas Folkways
Nancy McDonough

Coward, McCann & Geoghegan
200 Madison Avenue,
New York, N.Y. 10016

Acknowledgment is gratefully extended to the following
for permission to reprint from their works:

Citadel Press, Inc.: From "Go Tell Aunt Rhody" from *Folk
Music: USA* by Howard Grafman and B. T. Manning.
Copyright © 1962 by Howard Grafman. Reprinted by
permission of Citadel Press.

Doubleday & Company, Inc.: From "The Bee-boy's Song"
from *Puck of Pook's Song* by Rudyard Kipling. Reprinted by
courtesy of Doubleday & Company, Inc.

LSU Press: From "Buy Me a China Doll" and "The Storm
of Heber Springs" from *A Singer and Her Songs* by Almeda
Riddle (edited by Roger Abrahams). Copyright © 1970 by
Almeda Riddle. Reprinted by permission of LSU Press.

The Ozarks Mountaineer: From "We're Coming Arkansas" from *Songs of the Ozark Folk* by Leo Rainey. Copyright
© 1972 by Leo Rainey, Olaf and Orilla Pinkston.
Reprinted by permission of The Ozarks Mountaineer.

All efforts have been made to trace the original copyright
holders of all material in this book. If unknowingly we
have omitted proper acknowledgment, we hope those
concerned will contact us so that corrections can be made
in the next edition of the book.

To Lee Anne and Russell

CONTENTS

A NOTE ON THE TITLE—AND OTHER TITLES THAT MIGHT HAVE BEEN

"Garden sass" is a mountain term for a dish of fresh vegetables—tomatoes, cucumbers, green onions, etc.—served perfectly plain and ungarnished. It is the salad straight from the garden—washed, cut up, and put on a plate with no sauce or dressing of any kind. This book is like a plate of garden sass.

It is a collection of the customs our family has seen and the stories we have heard as we traveled the country roads of Arkansas. The photographs were never posed and the stories were left in the language "exactly as she was spoke." One old man that we met said about another, "He fixed up a lot of words different from the original," but I would not have dared that. This book would not have been garden sass if I had.

Most of all it is a happy book because it is about contented people. There is a saying that "He who laughs lasts" and certainly that is true of the older people of Arkansas. These are people who long ago made their peace with the land and have found their joy in the simple life. But another title could have been *Arkansas—Land of Transition;* for life in the hills is rapidly changing. The winding dirt roads are becoming four-lane highways. The Elizabethan English is being standardized by television. Electric cables and telephone wires are crisscrossing the forests. In some formerly remote areas it is easier to find a taco stand or a pizza parlor than it is to find a restaurant with good home-cooking.

The old ways are dying and the pulse of life is beginning to flow faster and faster. But a persistent traveler who is willing to go (as Vance Randolph said) "Up hills an' down hollers, crost branches an' through berrypatches," can still find an old man tending his bee gums, little old ladies quilting by a potbellied stove, and a lovely log cabin holding its head up proudly. Best of all he will find people so friendly and so unhurried that he will feel that he has always been a part of them.

He will also discover some unusual results as the old ways give place to the new. Here are some that we have encountered or heard of:

—Jimmy Driftwood told about the time the crew from a national magazine came down to photograph a "life in the hills" type of article. They were taking pictures of an old log cabin and kept wondering about the significance of some bedsprings that were nailed up on the roof. Finally the old man who lived in the cabin explained to them that those rusty springs were his TV antenna.

—Once I was photographing a family making molasses at an old sorghum mill out in the middle of a field. During the afternoon we saw a well-dressed woman carefully picking her way through the field. She turned out to be the neighborhood Avon lady—coming to "call."

—We have often seen people gathered around their wood-burning stoves watching television, or found saddle horses hitched up at gasoline stations. And once, when we were driving down a remote dirt trail into (aptly named) Hemmed-in-Hollow, we saw the final inroad of civilization. On a tree by the side of the trail someone had posted a hand-lettered sign saying INCOME TAX SERVICE with the preparer's name below.

But perhaps this transition can best be illustrated in these statements by an elderly black woman near Scott. Her washpot had coals under it and showed signs of recent use so I asked her if she still washed her clothes in it. She said, "No'm. I uses it to boil the water to put in my washing machine." Then we went out to her smokehouse, which she assured me she still used; but when I opened the door there wasn't any meat inside. When I asked her where all the meat was, she told me, "Oh, when I gets done smokin' my meat I puts it in my deepfreeze." That is the way it is in Arkansas today.

Which brings me to another possible title, *Finding Folklore is Fun.* In fact it is not only fun and exciting, but a marvelous educational experience as well. With as much prior knowledge as you can obtain, plus a camera, tape recorder, and a smile—you can help collect it. All around us there are living links with the past that will soon be gone. Often these people do not even realize that the ballads they sing or the homes where they live represent a vanishing part of our heritage.

What is unusual to some outsiders may be such an everyday occurrence to the native that he is amazed by their interest. In his book, *In Ireland Long Ago*, Kevin Danaher told about the old Irish custom of loading a donkey's back on either side with large baskets to carry the turf out of the bogs. This was a custom that was becoming rarer all the time and one that many people had never seen. Once, a Dublin man visiting in Kerry saw this and said, "'Excuse me, can I take a photo of your donkey with the baskets, for I never saw the like before?' Replied the Kerryman, 'You never saw one before? Oh, man, you must be from a very backward part of the country!'"

As you collect the folklife around you, you will also be collecting wonderful memories. How could we ever forget the easygoing people who have hung a sign on their business doors, saying OUT TO LUNCH or GONE TO THE POST OFFICE and then hopped in their jeep to take us out in the hills to see an old log cabin. Or the hospitality of others who have insisted that we come in to "set a spell" and drink iced tea, or stay for a marvelous dinner cooked on a wood-burning stove.

Sometimes you may have to search hard. However, in our state we have found that the rougher the road was getting to a community, the more likely it was that the folklife would be authentic when we got there. It is true that there are some barriers that you won't be able to leap. Once we went to a community looking for old stories and were told that the week before they had buried a ninety-six-year-old man who had lived there all his life, had a wonderful memory, and been a marvelous storyteller. No one had ever taped him. We were disappointed, but a neighbor cheered us up by telling us about another old man who lived nearby, was also a great storyteller, and was very much alive and kicking.

When we got there we discovered that he was a spry and articulate eighty-seven years old; despite the fact that he claimed, "I was pretty rough when I was a young man. I used to get pretty full and be the meanest man you ever seen. My pa told me a hundred times I'd never live to be fifty years old." But when we told him that his neighbor had recommended him as a good storyteller he looked shocked. In indignation he replied, "You tell him if he thinks I'm out tellin' stories you tell him he's wrong! I 'fessed religion here about two weeks ago and I'm thankin' my Lord for my troubles. I promised my Lord and my God if he'd take me out of them hospitals and let me go home to my wife that I'd be a better man and never tell stories, act wild, or drink whiskey no more."

After that we heard a lot about his conversion to the Lord, his stay in the hospital, and his good wife; but he never slipped up and told us even one little anecdote. Therefore, this is my plea to "gather ye folklore while ye may." You never know when technology, death, or " 'fessin religion" may snatch some knowledge away.

There is one last title that I could have chosen—something like *Folklore for Scholars and Lovers*. It would explain the way this book is written. I have tried to make the book interesting enough for anyone, young or old, to simply read and enjoy; and yet I have attempted to document it with enough names, dates, and places, to please the most exacting professor. You might say I was like the old

woman in Yell County who had her picture made for the
first time. Afterward, she turned to my grandmother and
said proudly, "I tried to look solemn with a smile on my
face."

At a typical country dinner, with fried chicken, ham,
gravy, three kinds of bread, and six cooked vegetables, the
garden sass is often the most refreshing part of the meal. I
hope this book will be just as delicious to you.

*Times are changing! Because of an old belief that crows are
afraid of snakes, farmers used to paint wooden snakes and
place them in their fields. This one was a piece of river
driftwood, painted by Elmer Moody many years ago, and
used in the fields of Stone County. Today, farmers buy rubber
snakes at the dime store and put them in their gardens to use
as sure-fire "scarecrows." Like so many folk customs, the
belief lingers on but the methods have changed.*

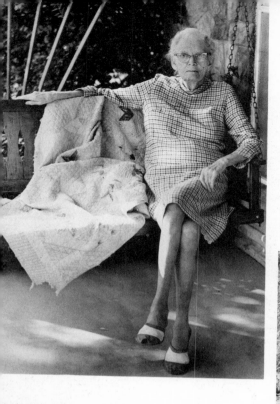

Mr. Bettis, Dan, and a "gee-whiz."

CHAPTER 1
ALONG A COUNTRY ROAD

Driving along the country roads of Arkansas, an observant traveler can see a wealth of folklife. In the distance there are Indian mounds rising up in the middle of a field and beside the road there are "council trees" where the Indians used to gather. Everywhere there are signs of the farmer's struggle for existence and the traditional ways he has carried on this struggle; the fences surrounding his land, the scarecrows guarding his fields, the homes and outbuildings he has built, and even the farmer himself, out plowing with his horse.

To enjoy true folklife the first step is to find a road "where traffic is noted for its absence." You can take your choice of such colorful names as Hog Thief Trail, Pigeon Roost Road, Ragweed Valley Road, Happy Hollow Road, and Soda Valley Road. You can travel the Old Wire Road (so named because of the early telegraph wires that followed it) or you can get on any of the old military roads that still cover the state. These latter roads got their name from the fact that they were built by the government to defend the frontier when Arkansas was still a territory.

The military roads, like the Wilderness Road and other early trails, were cut out of the woods along the paths of the old Indian traces. Early travelers described these as "obscure paths" and in the 1830's one writer told how the local men would remove the trees to make a road, but "holes and other hindrances are left in a state of nature, if there is the slightest chance that a wagon can pass."

In spite of the "hindrances" these were the roads that opened up the state for the early settlers and for people on their way to California to search for gold. Today a traveler can follow the well-marked Ozark Frontier Trail or take off on an obscure lane and enjoy some of the following sights without ever leaving his car.

COUNCIL TREES

All over the state there are enormous old trees that the local people claim were Indian council trees. Typical of these are the large oaks on the banks of the river at Dardanelle. The following legend is told about these particular trees:

In 1818 the first band of Cherokees traveled over the trails from the east and settled in the Arkansas territory. To keep the tribe intact they needed an assembly point for important occasions and tribal conferences. They chose for this purpose these enormous oaks growing beside the Arkansas River near the large Dardanelle Rock.

It was there that they met with Robert Crittenden, the acting governor of the Arkansas Territory, in 1823. The purpose of this conference was to arrange an agreement for the Indians to yield a large part of the land that they occupied south of the Arkansas River. Crittenden was there to induce the Cherokees, led by Chief Black Fox, to give up their homes and move north of the river, where they had land granted to them by treaty.

Over a hundred chiefs and tribesmen attended the council and a number of trees were felled to make seats for all of them. Robert Crittenden was sitting on one of the fallen trees when Chief Black Fox came over and sat beside

One of the council oaks at Dardanelle.

him. Black Fox repeatedly asked Crittenden to give him a
little more room on the log and the governor would move
farther down each time.

Finally Crittenden became angry and stated that he had
reached the end of the log and there was no more room.
Quietly Black Fox replied, "That is just the way with us.
Our great father has moved us from place to place until we
can go no farther."

Despite his eloquence the Cherokees were moved to the hills of northern Arkansas where they remained until their removal to Oklahoma. In 1838, when their fellow Cherokees were forced to leave Georgia, the Arkansas Indians joined them on the trip to Oklahoma; and the Indian traces became the Trail of Tears.

FENCES

During the following years the Trail of Tears became the Frontier Trail as the state was opened up for white settlement. Roads, homes, and towns were built across the land where once the Indians had roamed. Surrounding these fields, cabins, and outbuildings were the fences that farmers made to enclose their land. Today, when "bob-wire" is the standard material for most fences, it is fun to find some of the old rock, split rail, and paling fences still standing along a country road.

Probably the earliest of these were the rock walls that wind up and down so many of the hills. This custom of taking rocks directly from the fields for the marking of properties was practiced by the settled farmers of the Bronze and Iron cultures, and was brought by the early settlers from England. To begin these walls a large post was driven in the ground at the place where the gate was to be. Then, as the land was cleared, the rocks were stacked three or four thick beside the post and soon a wall was formed.

Those old stone walls would seem to be imperishable. But today many of them are disappearing as construction companies buy them, tear them down, and sell the beautiful moss-covered, weathered rocks to home-builders. So even these sturdy rock fences are fast becoming a part of our disappearing folk heritage.

Another early fence was the split rail, which was usually made of the trees that had also been cleared from the land.

Stake and Rider.

A pioneer rock wall (Newton County).

The logs were split into rails eight to twelve feet long and then fitted on top of each other in a zigzag pattern. This design gave rise to names like snake fence, worm fence, and Virginia crook fence. Despite these names, the zigzag was not haphazard. The line for the fence was marked off from corner to corner and a median line was carefully followed, so that the laying of a "straight" crooked rail fence was an achievement to be proud of. The main requirement was that it be "Horse high, hog tight, and bull strong"; or as another old saying goes, "Ten rails will keep out any reasonable farm animal, and you'll need a few extra rails for any unreasonable ones."

Gerstaeker, one of the state's first tourists (1830), noted that "The farmers are careful to use only the best wood in making rails." In fact, only a certain section of the tree was used for making rails. Colonel Buxton discussed this when he told about the time he and a friend split rails as "pay" for a neighbor's help in building a dugout canoe:*

> Chester and I wanted a dugout so we went over to Old River Island. We had friends over there—Jake Underwood and Will Taylor—who had made dugouts and had all the paraphernalia and the tools. Will Taylor offered to give us a cottonwood tree if we would cut the butt-cut off and make rails for his field from it. Then we could have the next two cuts. The butt-cut was the rail cut. We cut that and split it into rails and that was his pay for the tree, and for helping us, and for board—we stayed with him two or three days.

When sawmills became common the board fence came into popularity; and after 1867, when the first patent for a fence with "defensive points" was issued, the barbed-wire fence took over. It is possible that the early settlers also made fences out of mud, because the expression "ugly as a mud fence" is used all over the state; and out of brush, since an early ballad mentions the Arkansas settler with his

---

*In the St. Francis "Sunk Lands" (a swampy area of eastern Arkansas) the people traveled in dugout canoes even in this century.

A split-rail fence surrounds a pasture (Cleburne County).

A farmer didn't have to choose between rocks and rails. He could use both.

Mending fences, a springtime chore.

A "bedstid" makes a gate.

"tar-pole wagon and old brush fence"; but neither of these are seen today.

When it came to fashioning a gate for all these fences, the farmer was a great person to make do with whatever was handy. An old bedpost, the side of a wagon, bedsprings, or anything else the right size suited him fine. He was anxious to get the fields enclosed and get on with the business of farming.

SCARECROWS

Guarding over the precious crop that the farmer had worked so hard to plant was usually a scarecrow. This old custom, brought over by the English settlers, is still in evidence along the country roads. Like his ancestor, today's scarecrow is made in the shape of a cross. He is usually given a head with a floppy hat, and a suit of appropriate (or inappropriate) clothes. Attached to the hands are sometimes tin cans, pie pans, little mirrors, etc. that shine and move to help fool the crows; and Walter

Women's Liberation comes
to the fields.

The November rain drips
from his hat, and the corn
is gone, but this fellow
goes on guarding his field.

Mr. Wilhite's scarecrow
"for those crows that can read."

Moody told about the time his brother Kermit made a scarecrow that even had a gun in its hands.

In recent years farmers have discovered the practice of coating their seed with foul-smelling, bad-tasting products that discourage moles, crows, and other pests—without affecting the plant's growth. So scarecrows are becoming scarcer and scarcer, as another work of folk art disappears.

EVERLASTING SPRINGS

The pride of most localities is the nearby "everlasting spring," that is so named because it flows the year round. In the old days travelers often stopped there for a drink of water and as Roy Simpson said, "We always stretched out and drank on the ground." He went on to tell the story about the preacher who stopped for a drink at the spring on a Saturday afternoon:

You know how preachers were supposed to love chicken in those days. Well, a preacher stretched out on the ground and drank from the deep spring—and lost his false teeth

Kermit and Russ get a drink from the "fountain" on Cajun Creek Road (Stone County).

down into the spring. There he was, going to preach the next day, and he couldn't eat or preach without those teeth. And then he got an idea. So he hunted up a chicken bone and tied it to a string and lowered it down in the spring—and the false teeth clamped on it—and he just dragged 'em out.

Lying down on their stomachs to get a drink of water was as hard on other people as it was on the preacher. Over their springs the English people built elaborate permanent fountains commemorating various historic events. In Arkansas people used more primitive (and more ingenious) methods of creating drinking fountains. Brandy Baswell told how, in Heber Springs, they always stretched out on their stomachs to get a drink—until someone thought of putting a hollow gum stump upright into the ground and letting the water flow out of the top. Sulphur formed on the wood and left just a little spot flowing in the center.

Today the ferries are designated by highway markers (notice the 9), but they retain their colorful old names.

An even simpler solution is sometimes found today along a country road. A local farmer, who passes that way often and stops frequently at the spring, will drive a stick in the ground and put a tin can on the end to be used as a cup by any travelers along the road. This was a custom that began before the days of service stations, and it is still a nice type of drinking fountain to find on isolated country lanes.

FERRYBOATS

Sooner or later most country roads come to a stream or a river. Some cross the water with a conventional bridge, a wooden bridge, a low-water bridge, or a one-lane bridge. These are often picturesque; but even more exciting are the roads that cross on "floating bridges" or ferryboats. In

the old days the *Arkansas Gazette* was filled with advertisements like this one:

Wright Daniel's FERRY,
Four Miles Below Little Rock
The subscriber respectfully informs Travelers and others, that he still continues his old FERRY, across the Arkansas River, four miles below the town of Little Rock, at the following rates:
For a large wagon and team, ... $1.00
Wagon with two horses, ... 75
Wagon or cart, with one horse, ... 50
Man and horse, ... 12½
Footman or loose horses, ... 6¼
Each head of cattle, ... 6¼
Hogs and sheep, per load, ... 50
    Travelers can be supplied with CORN, at 50 cents per bushel, at the Ferry.
                                                          WRIGHT DANIEL
Four miles below Little Rock
June 28, 1825

Aunt Chat Standridge recalled how her father ran a wooden ferryboat that had log rails on the side and was powered by the current pushing the boat against the wire guide that ran across the river. Operated in that same primitive way is the Sylamore Ferry on the White River. Also guided by that method is the Wild Hawes Ferry that crosses the White River near the old Wild Hawes Steamboat Landing. The steamboats stopped at this landing in the early days when they made trips up and down the river, and the name came from the wild haw trees growing along the banks.

    Farther down the White River is the Oil Trough Ferry, with a paddlewheel on the side. The name for this ferry, and for the town of Oil Trough, came not from crude oil but from bear grease. In pioneer times people in the area killed hundreds of bears and shipped the grease down the

A two-story dog-trot house.

The cabin itself was usually put together at a neighborhood house-raising. People from all around came to help since the logs were heavy, and lifting large logs on top of each other was impossible for just one man. On the day of the house-raising whole families came, with the men bringing their axes and the women bringing their best food for the noontime meal. A long dinner-table and benches were improvised on the spot and fires were made so that the women could boil the coffee and cook the food.

As one man recalled, the women all gossiped and caught up on the news—then the older ones began to discuss religion, and the young ones began to discuss the young men. During the morning hours some women quilted while the others cooked; and during the afternoon, when most of the logs were in place, the women and children began the "mudding." That night, according to Roy Simpson, "the completion was celebrated by a dance in the

Sometimes the balance was precarious.

cabin during which corn liquor flowed more or less freely."

At the Willow House two ladies told me that, "The men in the community would all get together and build a house for somebody. They'd cut the logs and roll 'em in; drag 'em in; and build a house in a day." But Farmer Wilhite remembered that in Montgomery County the houseowner did some of the preliminary work:

The feller that is gonna have a house, or a barn, or whatever they are agonna build, he gets out the logs and peels them, and then he has his foundation there—rocks or whatever—to put the sills on. Then the neighbors'll all come in and they'll have a house-raising. And they raise the walls of this house so that it's up higher than your head. Then, it's up to the fellow that owns the house—he'll take a broadax and get inside and he hewes down the inside walls. After that is all done they get the roof framed where these walls will stand up good.

Once that much was completed the owner of the cabin could finish the house as he had time. There were choices to be made as to the type of floors, fireplace, etc.; and as you explore log cabins you will begin to notice these various details that help to tell each cabin's story.

FLOORS

As soon as possible the pioneer graduated from a dirt floor to a rough-hewn puncheon floor, and finally to a sawed plank floor. The dirt floor was just what its name says—the bare earth, which became packed and hard through the years. John Gideon said they had a dirt floor in their cabin and "every few weeks it was wet down and tamped." There are very few people left who even remember these. Fred High recalled visiting an old man who lived in a cabin with a dirt floor where the "table and stove set on a mound of dirt and could not be moved or they would turn over, as the dirt had worn out where they set." He also remembered that this man couldn't sweep anything out of his door since the bottom log (a round one) sat right on the ground and was a foot high.

The next step up was a puncheon floor. This was made from split logs that were placed side by side with the round side down. When they were added to an existing cabin with a dirt floor they were simply pressed into the earth and wedged together. However, most of the cabins were built with the puncheon floors as part of the plan and in that case the puncheons rested on the foundation logs. Farmer describes how they were placed in a well-built cabin:

Now, you see, they find some straight saplings about six inches in diameter and they split 'em right down the middle. And they line them with a line so's to split 'em just as accurate as they can. And where they cross a sill or a sleeper* they cut 'em off there, so they'll be the same width or thickness up here. And then when they put 'em down, now, *they don't fasten 'em.* And then they take a hand ax and work the edges so they lay close together. And then for the final windup of 'em, they push two together and they take a saw and run there between one and the other for a fine fitting. And then when they get that done why of course they'll be as rough as the dickens. Well, they take the foot adze and then they work across them crossways, and by being careful that makes a pretty good floor.

However, there were disadvantages to the puncheon floors. For one thing, as Farmer can testify, they warped.

I was at a dance one time and I don't remember whether we were playin' Virginia Reel or what it was, but I was havin' to back up. I was comin' backwards. And this was a rather old cabin and the floors—these puncheons—had warped and kinda tipped up there. So the edge of one was above the other one. And as I was a-backin' up I hung my heel on that higher puncheon and I just fell flat a my back. It like to knocked the dickens outta me!

Another disadvantage to a puncheon floor was the pulling apart that eventually came with age. This led to big cracks, and in some cabins people could remember looking down and seeing the chickens pecking beneath the house; or as someone once put it, "They could study geology through the floor." However, this problem could be corrected as long as the puncheons weren't fastened down when the house was built. Farmer explains how:

The puncheons—they're usually green when they're put in there. After awhile, why, they'll dry and shrink and there'll be cracks in there. Well, you see, they just drive wedges between two of 'em and spread 'em apart and if

---

*These terms, "sills" and "sleepers," refer to the foundation logs. As he explained, "The big ones on the ends would be sills and the intermediate ones would be sleepers."

they gain enough across the room why then they can take a thin piece and drive it down in between there so's to make the floor—well, where the children won't fall through, anyhow.

Sometimes the cracks came in handy. In the *History of Lawrence, Jackson, Independence and Stone Counties, Arkansas,* a man told this story:

> When a house was built a hole was dug under the hearth for the chimney. This left a hole under the floor to keep the sweet potatoes in.   One day my grandmother saw a panther coming. She lifted the puncheon floor and went down into the potato hole. The panther came into the house and stuck its claws down through the cracks of the puncheon floor. She cut off its toes with the hatchet.*

Because the disadvantages far outweighed the advantages, people were anxious to replace their puncheons with better floors. As communities developed, sawmills became common and people covered their rough floors with sawed planks. This makes it hard to find a puncheon floor inside a home today, but sometimes they can be seen on porches of the very old cabins.

DOORS AND WINDOWS

Impossible as it may seem, the doors, windows, and fireplace openings were usually cut out after the logs were up. It was decided ahead of time where they were to be and as a log was placed on the top side of that space the men took a saw and made cuts partly through the log, the width of the door or window opening. When the walls were up the owner could stick a saw through those cuts and saw right down to the bottom. The important part was

*For similar stories see the section on Hunting and Wild Animal Tales.

The stepstone.

A lock wasn't necessary.

to get the logs up while there were helpers available, and save the detail work for later.

After the opening was sawed down, doorjambs were fitted into the sides of the door space. These were put into place and a hole was bored through the jamb and into the log. Hardwood pins that had been seasoned, so that they wouldn't shrink anymore, were fitted into the holes to hold the jambs in place. Pins were used because nails were scarce and because most people felt that pins would hold tighter and wouldn't rust and rot the beams. In front of the door they usually placed a large rock called a stepstone. The first door was often a blanket or quilt, followed by a slab door with wooden, iron, or leather hinges. A letter written by a man in 1876, telling about the early days in Arkansas, said that, "If any man had had a lock on any of his doors in those days he would have been looked on with suspicion."

Glass windows were a luxury that most Arkansans could not locate or afford. As a substitute they used animal skins, greased paper, or wooden shutters. Aunt Chat said that the cabin where she was raised had wooden shutters that often had to be closed at night because of the mosquitoes and bugs. She said that made a house unbelievably hot on a summer night. For that reason many people moved their beds outside and slept in their yards or on the porch during the summer months. One woman showed me the deserted log house where her parents had lived and pointed to the spot in the front yard where her father had died in his bed asleep. When I asked what he was doing out there she looked amazed and said, "Why, it was summertime."

When the shutters weren't closed the bugs and flies were a real problem. Aunt Alma recalled going to a wedding dinner at an old cabin that had a lean-to kitchen with a dirt floor and no glass or screen for the windows. Big tables of food had been set up in the kitchen and children were stationed all around the tables, brushing the flies away with tree branches.

You can see how the turkey-feather roof got its name.

ROOFS AND LOFTS

Slats made with a shingling froe were an English custom that the pioneers brought with them. The turkey-feather roof (so named because of the way the shingles overlapped like feathers) was the standard roof on early log cabins.

With his froe and his wooden mallet the pioneer split his shingles and then laid them on his rafters. According to superstition he did this during the dark of the moon so that the shingles wouldn't curl as they dried. Today there are still many shingled roofs on houses and barns all over Arkansas. Some have been replaced with tin roofs which are not half as attractive, but make up for their lack of beauty by having a wonderful sound on a rainy night.

Almost all homes had sleeping lofts that were reached by a peg ladder on the inside of the cabin, or by a stepladder on the outside leading up to an outside door. The children slept in this half-story, and when the roof wasn't tight the snow would sometimes drift in on them at night (so the same children who could study geology through the floor were able to study astronomy through the roof).

Splitting shingles with a froe.

Sometimes the shingles came clear down the side of the house, as in this old cabin in Newton County.

SMALLER DETAILS

Once you have observed all the major points of the log cabin it is time to look at some of the details. On all the old cabins there will be adze marks on the hewn logs that will tell you by the way they are spaced how careful the workman was who hewed the logs. At the end of each log there are various types of notches where the logs fit together. The most common styles are the dovetail notch, the square notch, and the saddle notch; but it is fun to look for unusual types. Sometimes you will find a house where half the logs are of one style and half are of another, even on the same wall. Each workman apparently had his preference and followed it.

Between the logs there was chinking made of mud or clay, with animal hair, moss, or straw mixed in it. Roy Simpson explained that in the Ozarks and along the Fourche they had limestone which they burned and mixed with water to make a mortar. But he emphasized that, "There is no concrete about a true pioneer log house. If you ever see one with concrete about it, somebody's tampered with it."

Hard rain would wash the daubing out, and Fred High recalled that in the fall his family would have to replace the chinking in all the walls except the one that was protected by the porch. Sometimes slats were nailed on the outside to protect the chinking from the weather. To find the original mud chinking in most old log cabins the best place to look is right under the roofline where the "dobbin'" was protected by the overhang of the roof. If sticks or rocks were mixed in with the mud they will sometimes still be wedged between the logs, with all the supporting material gone.

Many of the one-room cabins had lean-to kitchens added in later years. You can tell right away whether the builder was superstitious or not when you look into this room. If there is not a door between the main house and the kitchen you know that he probably believed in the old mountain superstition that it was bad luck to cut a doorway between two rooms after the house was built.

Some builders were not so careful when making their notches.

This cabin, built by Cecil Murray's grandfather more than one hundred years ago, has overhanging dovetail notches.

There are other personal touches that have a story to tell. Occasionally a log will be placed at a right angle, below the others on one wall. This was usually added in later years to "level" the house. Mr. Cecil Murray showed us the log cabin his grandfather built over a hundred years ago. Mr. Murray's mother, who was born in 1890, told him that when she was a little girl her father kept talking about the fact that the house leaned to one side. One day her father propped up one side of the house and added an extra log on that side. When his mother told him which corner of the cabin had been raised, Mr. Murray went to the spot and discovered the log exactly where it had been placed almost eighty years before.

One of the biggest mysteries to a log cabin explorer is the tremendous number of neatly drilled auger holes in the sides of the cabins. These appear all over the house—on the inside and outside walls, up high and down low, carefully spaced and at random. There are many answers to the mystery and all of them have a story to tell about the pioneer and his traditional ingenuity. Here are some of the explanations given to us:

1. When the early settler headed West he could bring very little furniture, and he often had to leave the beds behind. But this was one of the first pieces of furniture he needed in the new land; so, as he built his cabin he made two holes in the wall for every bed he needed. Side rails were put into these holes and legs were placed at the other end, with the wall of the cabin becoming the headboard of the bed. Ropes were strung between the rails to hold the cornshuck ticks and feather beds. When this same type of bed was built into a corner it was called a "one-poster" since only one leg was needed.

2. Some of the holes on the outside were put there by the builders, who put pins in them to heist the heavy logs to the top.

3. Holes going neatly up the inside of one wall usually contained pegs that made a ladder to the loft. Holes

scattered at random on the inside walls often held wooden pegs for hanging clothes, frying pans, etc. There was little floor space, and no closets, so everything possible had to hang on the wall.

Pegs fitted into auger holes were for hanging.

In describing an Arkansas log cabin of the 1830's Gerstaeker mentioned, "Over the door were two wooden pegs supporting the long-rifle belonging to the man of the house. The bullet pouch and the powderhorn, two necessities in a hunter's life, hung suspended from one of the rifle pegs."

4. Inside or outside, the holes might indicate the place where pegs were put to hang the skeins of woolen thread. While describing an old log building, Aunt Chat said, "It had the warpin' bars on the front and everybody in the country come to our house to warp their thread, you know." Then she explained what warping bars were. "They was just big long pegs—they was this long [about a foot] and they was holes bored in the logs and them put ever so often. And then they [the people working with the thread] went over the top and then they come under the bottom and they'd plait their threads with their fingers this way, and hang 'em over certain pegs."

5. But of all the explanations given for the holes in the cabins this one was the most ingenious. A storekeeper in Franklin County told us that during the Civil War, while the men were away fighting, the women of the Ozarks bored holes in the walls of their log cabins with large augers. In the holes they hid their most precious possession—their seed corn. They knew that without this corn there would be no crop the next year. Once a peg was stuck in the hole the corn lay safely inside, protected from the Jayhawkers and bushwhackers who ravaged the mountains and stole or destroyed everything else they could lay their hands on.

FIREPLACES

More than any other part of the house, the fireplace could tell us the tales of the family who lived there. For it was the center of activity from the time of the earliest settlers until the advent of gas and electricity in recent years.

If you check carefully around a "boxed-in" house, you can sometimes find the old logs. This house was boarded over everyplace except the dog-trot, where the logs were still exposed.

Often you can tell the date that a log cabin was last inhabited by the dates on its "wallpaper." This cabin is more than one hundred and thirty years old, but as the pictures on its wallpaper clearly show, it is still inhabited.

Because they were used for so many different purposes
the fireplaces were sturdy and large, often taking up most
of one end of the room. Today, when many of the old logs
have rotted, burned, or been blown away, the durable
rocks that made up the fireplace are often the only part
left of the pioneer cabin. A verse in an old ballad describes
what has come to be a common and melancholy sight in
Arkansas—a house that has tumbled down and left a
lonely fireplace standing:

>Granny and I and Poll and Neil
>Sat in the room a'spinnin':
>Half the house came tumblin' down
>   And left the chimney stannin'.

Even a lone fireplace can tell a story about the home and
its occupants. Like the three little pigs, the early builders
had a choice of materials to use. Some of the earliest
frontiersmen used "sticks and daub" to make their
chimney; others used rock; and in some of the best houses
bricks were used. (There was even a "half and half" style,
where the bottom part was stone and the top half was
mud.)

Both are still being built today, but a stick and daub
chimney has become a rarity. These were often called "cat"
chimneys, and Mr. Claude Lawrence, who has the remains
of a cat chimney on an old cabin at his homeplace,
described a cat as a ball of mud with a grass thread
running through it to hold it together. Roy Simpson called
it a big bologna sausage and said, "It was a mud brick just
like the children of Israel were making."

Farmer Wilhite explained exactly how a cat chimney was
made. First they gathered about "half a wagonload" of
grass, the finer the grass the better. Then they got their
mud, preferably from the creek bottoms. "There's a mud
they call 'post oak' mud. Now if you've got a field that's got
that in it why that's the stickiest stuff—you go to plow

through that and the mud'll just hang up on your plow like you're trying to plow through a bunch of toesacks. Well, you go down there and get that post oak mud, and when it gets hard and dry it's just almost like a brick." (Mr. Simpson, who was from the same region, called this "crawfish clay" or "post oak flat," and said that this was a white clay.)

If you weren't lucky enough to have post oak mud there was another solution. "Now they used to have mud mills—a thing that you hook a horse to and go round and around and round. It was kinda like a barrel and it had a stem going down through the middle, and paddles out around on this stem. And there was a gate down there at the bottom so that the finished mud would come out. And you'd have a little platform for it to come out on." (Mr. Simpson said, "Some folks got an old whiskey barrel and made a mill and had a horse mix it.")

When they didn't have a muddy field and didn't have a mud mill, Farmer Wilhite had one other solution. "Just make a box about four feet square and about a foot deep—and you get in there barefooted. Now you shovel in some of this dry dirt and you pour in water. Oh, the kids they think that's fun. Just roll up their britches and they can get in there and just squish around with their bare feet."

After they had their grass and their "chimney dirt" it was time to make the cats. Mr. Wilhite explained, "Now, it takes some experience to make these cats where they'll work right." First they nailed one end of a piece of canvas onto a table. Then they took a paddle and spread the mud on the canvas. Next they put a layer of grass on top of the mud and took hold of the loose end of the canvas to roll the mud and grass up like a jelly roll.

Four framing pieces were put up where the chimney was to be and sticks were nailed on the inside to form a frame. Starting at the bottom, the cats were piled up, with the sticks as support. "One feller made the cats and the

The collapse of a stick and mud chimney in the Ouachita Mountains.

other put 'em across it. At the same time a stone lining was put on the inside of the chimney and filled in plumb tight with mud. After you get up above where the heat of the fire will be you can leave off the inside rocks." When they were finished they put a row of rocks around the top of the chimney to keep the weather from beating off the mud. In spite of this, the fireplace collapsed if the house was left vacant. Once there were no more fires to keep the cats dry the rain turned them to mud; which explains why a stick and daub chimney is so hard to find today.

The stick and daub chimney was built almost exclusively in the pine log cabins of the Ouachita Mountains, while in the Ozarks the fireplaces were built almost entirely of rock. There is no good explanation for this that I know of. In explaining why they built cat chimneys Farmer Wilhite said, "People can build this kind of chimney that can't lay up a rock chimney." But were the people of the Ouachitas any less adept than the people of the Ozarks? Roy Simpson laughed as he related: "Somebody said, 'You built it I guess because you didn't have any rocks.' I said, 'No, we wore out the rocks stumbling around over them while we built the mud and stick chimney.'"

After either type of chimney was completed it was cured by building a large fire in it to dry out the lining. Then it was ready for its many uses. The crackling fire in the fireplace provided the only means of heat in cold weather and was often a major source of light. It was also the

A beautiful Ozark rock chimney on a cabin that is almost gone.

kitchen stove, since most of the cooking was done there in big iron pots, kettles, and skillets. Some of the earliest Southern dishes, such as hoecake, johnnycake, and "shortenin' bread," were originally cooked over the coals of the fireplace. By using the ashes from the fire the soap was made, and by using the heat as a forge the tools were mended.

Two large rocks usually served as "dog irons," and in front of the fireplace a large stone was placed as a hearthstone. In some of the more primitive homes or in less rocky areas the bare earth had to serve this purpose. Mr. Simpson explained that "the only trouble with a clay hearth was that as you swept it, it finally wore out."

Beside the hearth sat the item described in this old riddle:

> Long legs, crooked thighs,
> Bald head and no eyes. (Fireplace tongs)

It was on the hearth that the churn was placed for the milk to "turn"; the lightbread dough was put so it would rise; and the flatirons were heated for pressing the clothes. It was there that Grandma sat to rock the baby and there that the family gathered at bedtime for Bible reading and prayers.

Today, the work, prayers, and laughter are gone from around the fireplaces since many of the homes have disappeared. There are no crops to gather in the fields, no roofs for the trees to shade, and no children to pick the crape myrtle that continues to bloom. But if a traveler approaches the lonesome fireplace very quietly and listens very carefully he may still hear the creak of a rocking chair beside the hearth or catch a whiff of cracklin' bread cooking on the fire.

Old log cabins don't always die: They can get added onto, they can prop up billboards, or they can become barns— with trees growing out of the chimney. Sometimes they remain sturdy homes (next page), so all in all, a log cabin is a good place to live.

CHAPTER 3
OUTBUILDINGS AND THEIR LORE

Still standing near the lonesome fireplace will sometimes be a barn, a well, or some other outbuilding that escaped the fire or storm that took the house away. Even if the homes of early Arkansas were not too elaborate they were surrounded by enough other structures to make up for their simplicity. As soon as the pioneer had a roof over his head he began adding a barn, a corncrib, a well, a storm shelter, a springhouse, a smokehouse, an ash hopper, a fruit house, a turnip cellar, and some bee gums. Many of these can still be seen around country homes today and most of them are an important part of Arkansas folklife.

THE SPRINGHOUSE AND THE WELL

One of the first things the settler had to locate was a steady supply of fresh water. The earliest arrivals in the new land usually settled near an everlasting spring and built a springhouse over it, so they would have a good place to get clean water and a cool place to store their milk and butter. The water from the spring had to be hauled to

A lonely outbuilding.

the house unless the spring ran right through the yard,
which it did in some cases.

Sometimes the spring was used by several families and
was quite a distance from the house. One woman wrote me
the following account of her childhood days near the
Buffalo River: "MY mother kept her milk in the cold
spring hollor. I would go get it every meal. LOTS of
snakes. YOU know i did not even think of thim than.
NOW i would be so scard. we went bare foot all summer."
Because of the spring's inconvenient location (and maybe
because of the snakes) people all over Arkansas soon dug
wells to assure a good supply of water for themselves and
their stock.

The most important aspect in digging a well was
knowing where to dig, and surely the most fascinating
method of deciding *where* was by water witching. This was
an old custom brought over by the earliest settlers from
England and used by almost all pioneers to locate wells
throughout Arkansas. The idea has been traced far back

Wooden well in the Ouachita Mountains.

into ancient history. It was used as early as the fifteenth century in Germany and was at one time a common practice all over Europe, where it was denounced by many churchmen.

The ability to witch for water was a talent supposedly given to only a few people and one that was (and is) strongly believed in by many people. If the dowser held in his hands a live, forked branch from a particular tree and walked along the land holding a fork of the stick in each hand, with the main section pointing upward, he would feel the stick suddenly jerk toward the earth when the rod passed over water. At this point the diviner would begin to chant, pass into a state, have muscular spasms, or simply say, "Here's the water," depending on his personality.

There is an old saying that goes, "'Every man to his own opinion,' said the old lady as she kissed the cow." Never was this more true than in the choice of sticks used by the various dowsers. Some said the stick *had* to be from a peach tree, or a willow tree, or a hazel tree. Others said it

Walter Whitfield draws water from his well.

Stone well in the Ozark Mountains.

just had to be a fruit tree, or a tree that bore sour fruit.
Still others said that any green, forked stick would do. In
Sweden diviners used mistletoe. Today the most modern,
up-to-date witchers may use bent wires or welding rods
and one woman in Stone County even made it work with
coathangers. In case you want to try witching, Floyd
Holland claims "Two wires will work for pert near
everbody."

Some diviners could tell exactly how deep the water
would be by counting how many steps they took between
the time they felt the first pull and the greatest pull, or by
how many times the stick bobbed over the spot. Alonzo
Tallent, a water witcher in the Ouachita Mountains, told
his method of determining how deep the water was: "You
get your switch set and you start walking to hunt a vein.
And when you feel an attraction, well, you stop and make
a mark. And you go on until it falls. Then you step back to
your mark and if it's only eight steps it would be
twenty-four feet to water. Always multiply by three."
However, when I asked Floyd Holland, an Ozark dowser,
if he could estimate the depth, he said: "That's guesswork.
I never did guess at but one well and I missed it two foot.
They tell me as far as you can feel that switch draw, it's that
many feet to the water."

Even though he doesn't put too much stock in
estimating the depth with a stick, Mr. Holland is one who
believes that the rod will work for substances other than
water. As he put it, "Anybody that can witch for water, I
mean if the switch'll work for 'em; whatever you put in the
end of that switch it'll work to it. You can put a dime in
there and it'll work to silver; you can put a penny in there
and it'll work to copper. You got to put whatever you're
looking fer in the end a that switch. But it won't work to
water with any kind of metal in the end of the switch."

To sum it all up, Newman Sugg described his
experiences with water witching:

You either have it or you don't! You can take a forked peach tree stick, or a hickory—green, it has to be green, you know—and you can hold that up, and when it hits that stream, why *you can't hold it.* It'll go down! It doesn't matter how stout you are. I've seen Glenn, Pauline's husband, I've seen him hold 'em till they'd stick in his hands and they'd just twist right on down, you know.

The only time it ever worked for me—it scared me. They's a somethin' there you don't understand. Over here in this place where Troy Buckman was a-drillin' for this chicken farm, we were talkin' about that, and he said, "It's a gift." I said, "It won't work for me," and he said, "Well, I'll make it work." So he said, "It'll work the same way for a piece of metal if you've got a piece of metal of the same kind to put in the stick." So he threw a half a dollar down out over there on the ground aways and then he put a nickle in the end of that stick and walked over there and it just went right down.

So he handed it to me and said, "You try it." I said, "Glory, it won't work for me." He said, "I'll make it work." And when I started with that thing he got behind me and just laid his—he didn't touch my hands—he just put his hands, each one of 'em on my arms, now, and when that thing hit that—it really scared me now—that just went right down. There was a power there that I couldn't understand. Coming from him! It wouldn't work for me—I could of carried that thing up there all day.

Just a few days after, Glenn found out it would work for him. They sent Glenn to get an old man to locate a well for the school. He said the old man was sittin' out in a chair behind the house—it was summertime—and Glenn told him they wanted him to come locate a well. And the old man got up and drug off out there to a peach tree and cut off a limb—a two-forked limb—kinda like the wishbone of a chicken, that's the nearest I can describe it. He took that old switch and he went down there to the school and started walking around with that thing. Directly, down it went. And he circled around and come back and it was the same place. He said, "Well, you've got a strong one here."

He said, "You ain't gonna have to dig anywhere to get that," and said, "That's real close." And when they drilled it they got an artesian—it just run out.

Glenn come down here in a few days after that and Red hadn't had that well dug, he was havin' to haul a lot of his water for the chickens, and he usually would go get Gentry Keener—he was what you'd kinda call a professional at that [water witching].

So I told Glenn what he was gonna do and he said, "Let's go up there and see if I can locate it. Then we'll see how well Gentry comes out with me." So we went up there and he walked plumb around that chicken house, all the way around, and he was almost back and he was gettin' uneasy; and his stick jerked right down, you know. And he said, "Well, right here now—I don't know what's there but somethin' pulled it down." And I said, "Well, now, let's mark that spot," and we took a piece of this green shingles—roofin' shingles, you know—and I said, "Glenn, let's lay this thing down here, put a little rock on it, and we'll get Red to not mention it to Gentry." So Red come along while we were there and we showed him where it worked for Glenn and he said, "Well, I sure hope that's right"; he said, "That'd be in a good place."

But he went the next mornin' and got this Keener feller and he took him there to the gate and said, "There's the chicken house yonder. Be sure and find me some water." Well, he went in a big circle all the way around—I think he missed that one the first time, didn't get over far enough maybe—but he made another circle and he come right back there and down it went. And he says to Red, says, "Boy, you got a strong stream. Right here, Red. Here's a good place." Said, "You see this piece of roofin' here—just dig right there." Now that's the fact of that. And Lloyd dug that well, he drilled it seventy-two feet and cased it the same day, and I reckon you could irrigate the mountain with it. There's no limit to the amount of water.

And today there's no limit to the argument—does water witching work or not? Some people say you can find oil,

Alonzo Tallent, water witcher.

Polly Lancaster, water witcher.

detect criminals, cure diseases, predict ball scores, or dowse from a distance using a map. Others say it's all a big hoax. There is still a British Society of Dowsers and in the summer of 1972 an article in a London newspaper told how a lorry driver in Warwickshire had located some underground drains with his witch-hazel stick, after electronic equipment had failed in the search. Soon afterwards an AP aerospace writer reported that the

Apollo 17 astronauts would carry with them two "space age 'divining rods'" to sound for water below the surface of the moon.

Newman is a believer—"They's people'll tell you it won't work, but it does." Uncle Aaron Stevens is a doubter—"I don't believe in them water witchers. I just got out there and dug a hole. I think one person can see as deep under the ground as another." And Brandy Baswell hedges with, "Yeah, it worked, sure. Mighta been water there anyhow without the stick, but it worked."

So, call it what you will—water witchin', switch twitchin', dowsin', or divinin'—people have believed in the power of the rod for hundreds of years, and there are many people in Arkansas who wouldn't dream of digging a well without using a rod today.

Floyd Holland, water witcher.

Sam Hess said his wife's great-grandfather built this smokehouse before the Civil War. The beams where the meat was hung were made of cedar logs.

THE SMOKEHOUSE

After the well was built the settler's next concern was with the preservation of food. One of the most important of his outbuildings, and the only one providing storage for meat, was the smokehouse. Bear, deer, turkey, and other game were smoked, but the chief source of meat was the hog.

When a pioneer moved into a settled area he was often approached by the original settler, offering to sell him a "hog claim." This practice was explained by Farmer Wilhite:

> The stock all run outside—there was no stock law a-tall. And each settlement had what they called "hog claims." The hogs run wild and eat acorns and roots and bugs and stuff. For two dollars you could buy into this hog claim bunch there, and that gave you the right to the meat whenever they had a hog killing.
>
> You see, the hogs run loose in the woods. When it got winter and bad weather and the hogs couldn't get as much

Inside the smokehouse door you can see the old stump that served as the cutting block.

food as they needed, a feller on a mule would take some corn over to the spring and strew it around. He'd go every day, usually early of a morning; and that'd get the hogs baited and used to coming up to that place. The people'd choose a place close by a branch where they could get plenty of water to scald and dress out the hogs. They'd haul up some wood and scalding barrels over there ahead of time to get the hogs used to the wood.

Then, come a cold spell, a hog hunt would be organized. They'd get over there—the fellers with the Winchesters— they'd get in there and surround this place and when the hogs came in there to get the corn, then the shootin'd start. And they'd shoot down as many hogs as they thought they could tend to. The hunters would run in with the "sticking" knives and bleed the kill. Then they'd have the scalding barrel and the pots to heat the water in and they'd dress 'em out—out there—and then they'd divide up the meat.

And everybody'd go home and have some meat on the table.

An area that was sparsely settled had plenty of room for each farmer's hogs to roam "on the range." In that case most of the hogs had ear brands to mark their ownership and the brands were often recorded in the office of the county clerk. These range hogs were considered as mean as bears and led to the many tales about the razorback hogs of Arkansas. These razorbacks were supposedly descendants of hogs that were brought to Arkansas by De Soto and that escaped into the woods to become gaunt animals that "were too thin to cast a shadow" and "had ridges on their backs so sharp they could be used as a razor." Most people agreed with Farmer Wilhite that "The most dangerous animal in the woods was an old rangesow with a litter of pigs."

When the stock laws came into existence the hog claims and the range hogs went out, but the butchering continued in the same manner as before. No matter where the hogs came from (wild or tame) they were killed in the winter and most of the meat was smoked for preservation. The bony parts, such as the ribs, were eaten right away since they spoiled so easily. Then the hams, shoulders, and bacon parts were hung up in the smokehouse. Fred High told how his family always removed the bones from the hams before smoking them, so that there would be less chance of spoilage. One time the Jayhawkers came through and as Fred told it, "They wanted some meat and of course they wanted the best. So they went in the smokehouse to help themselves and one was a man that could not talk plain. He was tossing the meat around on the bench and saying, 'Where is the hamps? I never saw a hog without hamps. Where is the hamps?'—as he did not know meats after the bone was taken out."

There were several steps to hog butchering that were standard and these are still practiced today. First of all the hogs to be killed were fattened on corn. After a few weeks they were taken out on a cold day to be slaughtered. This was usually a neighborhood affair. As Patience said,

"Folks'd come together and kill hogs. Kill my hogs today and yours tomorrow. You know, they'd have so many to kill." Unlike other "get-togethers" the butchering of the hogs was not a pleasant affair, but was a necessary one.

To see how little the ways of meat curing have changed, it is interesting to compare present-day accounts with the charming and succinct directions given in a cookbook published in 1824. Under the heading "To Cure Bacon," the author, Mary Randolph, gave the following directions:

Hogs are in the highest perfection, from two and a half to four years old, and make the best bacon, when they do not weigh more than one hundred and fifty or sixty at farthest; they should be fed with corn, six weeks at least, before they are killed. To secure them against the possibility of spoiling, salt them before they get cold; take out the chine or back-bone from the neck to the tail, cut the hams, shoulders and middlings; take the ribs from the shoulders and the leaf fat from the hams: have such tubs as are directed for beef. [She suggested these tubs be made from "a molasses hogshead," sawed in two, and raised on one side about an inch.] Rub a large table spoonful of saltpetre on the inside of each ham, for some minutes, then rub both sides well with salt, sprinkle the bottom of the tub with salt, lay the hams with the skin downward, and put a good deal of salt between each layer; salt the shoulders and middling in the same manner, but less saltpetre is necessary; cut the jowl or chop from the head, and rub it with salt and saltpetre. You should cut off the feet just above the knee joint; take off the ears and nose, and lay them in a large tub of cold water for souse. When the jowls have been in salt two weeks, hang them up to smoke—do so with the shoulders and middlings at the end of three weeks, and the hams at the end of four. If they remain longer in salt they will be hard. Remember to hang the hams and shoulders with the hocks down, to preserve the juices. Make a good smoke every morning, and be careful not to have a blaze; the smoke-house should stand alone, for any additional heat will spoil the meat. During the hot weather, beginning the first of April, it should be occasionally taken down, examined—rubbed with hickory ashes, and hung up again.

Compare those directions with these that were given to me by Walter Yardley on New Year's Day, 1972. As his wife passed around a bowl of cracklin's from the hog they had just finished butchering, Walter described the process. A big vat (in this case a tin barrel) had been filled with boiling water for scalding the hog. Walter said there were several ways to keep the water hot:

1. boil the water in other (smaller) vessels and pour it into the vat,

2. build a fire under the vat,

3. build a fire nearby around some big rocks and shovel these hot rocks into the vat.

This last suggestion was identical to the method described by Gerstaeker on his trip through Arkansas in the 1830's. He said, "Not having a pig kettle we were compelled to scald them in a typical Arkansas manner. A barrel, one end of which has been knocked out, is placed in a slanting position, half of it in the ground, and filled with creek-water. Nearby a huge wood fire is kindled in which are placed several large stones. When these stones begin to glow they are thrown in the barrel. In a few minutes the water reaches the desired temperature."

After the hog was dipped into the boiling water all the hair was pulled and scraped off. Walter used a regular garden rake to help with this process. The pig was hung up on a tree while the innards were taken out. In the old days a "gamblin' stick" (a hickory stick sharply pointed on each end) was inserted in slits in the hind legs to hold the hog up on the tree, but Walter said he now uses a chain pulley on the tree and a truck to pull the hog up.

The meat was cut into sections and put into barrels with salt packed all around it, filling in every crevice. It would be left there several days; then the salt would be brushed off. Some of the salt would be left on, depending on how salty they wanted it. The hog would then be hung in a smokehouse to cure it. The parts are hung from the rafters, and iron pots filled with burning hickory chips are put inside the smokehouse and kept burning (but not blazing) until the meat is cured. Alon⁻o Tallent thriftily suggested using a cracked washpot that was no longer good for washing to hold the burning wood. He also said the timing of the smoking period depended on the size of the hog. If it was "heavy fleshed" it would take longer. To test whether the meat was ready to stop smoking they would cut off a piece and cook it to see if it tasted just right.

The fresh wild game that was killed during the year and the hams hanging in the smokehouse made up most of the settlers' meat diet. However, a few exceptions were noted. Other meats that were available included:

Fresh Beef. Newman said that on Chickalah Mountain, "Most of the time when they'd kill a beef in the summertime, why they'd just dress it and they'd cut off what they wanted and they'd start peddling it out among the neighbors, you know. And maybe a week or two from then some other guy would kill one. By doing that in the community—somebody killing one ever week or ten days—they'd have fresh meat all summer." Another man said, "When we killed a beef we divided it out; everybody got some."

This practice, called "quartering," was used all over the state and was apparently an old British custom. Kevin Danaher reported that in Ireland an animal was "shared around among a circle of neighbors even if very little of it were salted down, and when each neighbor killed an animal in turn, fresh meat was had by all at fairly frequent intervals."

Jerky. Sometimes the meat was "jerked" to preserve it. This was especially true where a homestead was temporary and there was no smokehouse available. The meat would be seasoned and then laid on a latticework frame four or five feet off the ground. A slow fire was built underneath and the meat would be left there until it was thoroughly dried out.

Sausage. Patience said, "You know there's a great long piece of fat grows inside of the meat. You pull that off and take that and make sausage out of it. We'd put it in guts or little sacks and hang 'em up in the smokehouse and smoke 'em." Mrs. Wilhite said that her mother-in-law used to fry the sausage and then put it in a churn and pour the grease over it. This was called "lardin' it down" and meat fixed that way would keep all winter. As Patience said, "Back then, you know, things didn't spoil like they do now."

Souse. The feet and other parts were sometimes pickled in a salted brine, but according to Patience the best way to preserve them was to "Take the ears, and the head, and the feet, and make 'hogshead souse.' Just cook it all together—put your salt and sage and black pepper in the pot; and after it all gets real done you put it in a pan and take your hands and work all them bones and things out. You had to put it in a big pan and put some plates over it to pack it—and then you cut it."

No matter how they cured their meat, all Arkansans, both yesterday and today, have used the meat from the hogs to make two of their favorite kinds of gravy. With the ham goes "redeye gravy," and with the sausage goes "thickenin' gravy." Both of these are delicious as a sop for hot biscuits or cornbread.

Redeye gravy (also called speckled gravy and calico gravy) *—

Boiling water, mixed with strong black coffee, is poured into the skillet where ham has been fried. The liquid is stirred until it has mixed well with the juices and little bits of meat left in the pan.

---

*Here is one explanation for the way redeye gravy got its name. Supposedly, Andrew Jackson ordered his cook (who had been drinking heavily) to bring him some good, strong ham gravy. When he got the gravy Jackson remarked that it looked as dark as the cook's red eyes.

Thickenin' gravy (directions given by Lillie Sugg)—
"Cook your sausage. Take it up and leave the grease in
the pan. Put flour in the pan and brown it. Cook it for a
long time. Put milk in it and cook it a good while—until it's
good and thick."

THE FRUIT HOUSE AND THE TURNIP CELLAR

Since food preservation was one of his chief concerns,
the pioneer developed innumerable ways of solving the
problem. Two methods the early Arkansas settlers often
used for fruits and vegetables were a fruit house and a
turnip cellar.

In the early days a fruit house was usually hollowed out
of the side of a hill and was supported with logs and rocks.
Just being in the ground was supposed to keep the food
cool enough, and it usually did. Later, fruit houses were
built like cabins, with double walls packed with sawdust
between them. Even the door was packed with sawdust,
and a little hole with a roof over it was cut in the ceiling to
allow any hot air to escape. Inside both types of houses
there was a dirt floor and the walls were lined with shelves
for home-canned goods. In front of the shelves platforms
were built to hold the dried vegetables.

Before the fruits and vegetables were put into the fruit
house they were often preserved in some way. Here are
some of the most popular old methods:

Green Beans were usually "nipped" and strung on a
thread to make what most people call shuck beans or
"leather britches." They supposedly got this latter name
because they looked like a row of britches hanging on the
clothesline on washday. The leather came from their
toughness, for as Fred High said, "When the bean got
good and dry so it would keep for winter, it taken lots of
cooking to get it back to life." Polly Lancaster said her

family dried *okra* in the same way; and Aunt Chat said they shelled their beans before they dried them to "keep the weevils out."

Pumpkins were preserved in two ways. Jim Bixler recalled how "They'd make pumpkin butter in copper kettles—it'd take nearly all day to make a pot of that," and the kids would all hang around until the pumpkin butter began bubbling up and popping all over them.

Polly told how her mother sliced the pumpkins and

An early-day fruit house.

hung them on rods near the cookstove, adding that "They're a lot better dried in the house than they are in the sun." Farmer Wilhite said:

Nearly everybody raised pumpkins—by the wagonloads. Because they was all used up one way or another. To dry them you cut them crossways there, in rings. Hanging right next to the fireplace there was a framework hanging down—like the quilting frames used to hang down from the ceiling.

You'd cut these pumpkins in these rings, oh, about three quarters or an inch thick; then of course you'd peel off the outside hull part; and then you'd have sticks that you'd put these [pumpkin circles] on and set 'em up on this frame there—kinda like drying tobacco in the tobacco barns. And you'd put 'em up there and every day or two you'd turn 'em so it all dried uniformly all around. You utilized the heat from the fireplace. And that, now, is delicious when it's cooked.

And now, if you was going a-hunting or any trip on foot—you just take one of them big pieces of pumpkin, put in your coat pocket, and then you'd just bite off, or if you've got a knife—cut you off a piece and put it in your mouth and chew it and it's absolutely delicious.

He went on to say how much "our stock loved pumpkins." To preserve the pumpkins for the cattle, people would put a load of corn in the corncrib, then pile on one or two wagonloads of pumpkins and cover the pumpkins with more corn. This helped protect the pumpkins from a hard freeze, because frozen pumpkins would turn into mush when they thawed out.

Cabbage was preserved by cutting the heads into quarters and packing them in a crock with salt between the layers. This was covered tightly and allowed to ferment until it turned into sauerkraut. Today, Polly says that one woman sometimes brings an old-time dish of sauerkraut and dumplings to their church dinners.

Corn "was cut off the cob and strung like the bean" according to Fred High, but some people cut the corn off and dried it out flat on a scaffold with their fruit. Patience had whole ears of corn hanging next to her strings of dried red peppers, but she said they were "plantin' corn" not "eatin' corn."

Peaches and *Apples* were cut into slices and laid out in the sun to dry. Most people built scaffolds to hold their fruit up off the ground and to keep it away from animals. Lillie

Sugg said the best scaffold she ever had was an old screen
door, because the air could get to the fruit from both sides.
Paty said that "if you don't have a scaffold you can wash off
the roof and put 'em up on the roof." An old woman on
Weathers Mountain told me that she always dried her fruit
on the roof of the smokehouse. One advantage of the roof
was that it wouldn't collapse. Fred High recalled that,
"The folks would have peach and apple cuttings and
would gather in at night and cut them and tell Britt Tales.
[Britt was a local character.] One night a lot gathered into
a woman's and cut a lot of peaches and got the scaffold full
and it taken a tumble in the weeds and dirt."

Although people all over the state dried their fruit in
exactly the same way, they disagreed on how long it took to
dry it. Paty said, "Two days'll dry 'em—two days on that
roof," while Patience said, "Takes more'n a week or two."
Everyone agreed that the fruit had to be brought in at
night since "the night'd make 'em black" or "when the dew
gets 'em it makes 'em dark." For this reason Paty said, "It's
handier to put 'em on a sheet so whenever you want to
take 'em off you just roll the sheet up, you know, with the
fruit on it."

One other way to preserve fruit (peaches, strawberries,
persimmons, etc.) was to make "leather" out of it. The
pulp was pressed through a sieve, rolled out into a sheet,
and dried until it looked like a piece of leather. This was
cut into small pieces to use as it was needed.

Recently, the shelves of the fruit cellars have been filled
with home-canned goods, some of which are still cooked
on a woodburning stove. Many women wouldn't think of
canning on any other kind of stove. When Roberta
Wittenberg got a new electric stove she put her old
woodburner outside under the trees, where it would be
cooler to do the canning in the summer. Cooking outside
in the summertime is itself an old custom. Fred High
remembered, "My mama was the mother of four children
before she ever cooked on a stove. It was a skillet and lid,

Roberta Wittenberg's "canning stove."

in the winter by a fireplace. And in summer when it was too hot, it was under a tree."

Some people canned or dried their *potatoes* and *turnips,* but most people kept their root vegetables "under the ground, where they belong." To do this they built a root cellar, which was a simple and often temporary structure compared to the fruit house, which was more elaborate and permanent. Hilling the turnips was described by Newman Sugg:

> Well, the way they did that, they'd dig a hole or a pit like. And, of course, they'd throw the dirt out to the side and then they'd put in straw and hay—whatever they had—the mosta the time back then it was oats straw or somethin' like that. Then they'd put their turnips in and they'd lay these boards back over there, and put down somethin' like a tarp or a solid somethin' that wouldn't let the water run through. And they'd put that on there and then put their

dirt back on top of that. It was just a sort of a little storm cellar was what it was—they called it a hill or a pit. They had a little doorlike place dug there where they could put their straw and stuff over and just open up a small place. And they could reach back in there and get it [the vegetables]. It wasn't deep enough to get down in . . . . It would keep 'em most of the times all the winter.

Today, with the increase of canning and freezing, very few people dry their vegetables in the old ways. However, many farmers still hill their potatoes and turnips since a simpler method of protecting the root vegetables has not evolved; and fruit is still dried all over the state. Anyone who has ever eaten a dried apple pie will understand why.

Mrs. Kilgore's dried apples, hanging on the line.

The Storm Cellar

Closely related to the fruit cellar was the storm cellar. Sometimes they were one and the same, but people often built (and still build) a storm shelter strictly for protection from the many tornadoes that sweep over Arkansas in the early spring and fall. It is a large cellar dug out of the ground, with the sides supported either by timbers or rock walls. Around the oldest houses the shelters are usually mounded over with dirt taken out of the cellar; around later houses there are rock walls built up above the ground; and the most modern storm shelters are made of concrete.

Most of the people who have lived in the mountains for a long time have been in at least one bad storm, and for the rest of their lives they tend to date events as "before the storm" or "after the storm." One of the worst tornadoes to hit the state was the one that hit Heber Springs, a little town in the foothills of the Ozarks, on Thanksgiving Day, 1926. Forty-three people were killed in that storm and survivors remember it in great detail almost fifty years later. Brandy Baswell, age eighty-seven, told how the wind blew a two-by-four through a cow's stomach, and some other unusual results of the storm:

It blowed a broom handle through a gallon jug and didn't break the jug.

This family—there was nine in the family—it killed seven. They heard the tornado coming like a train. [One of the survivors in this family told Mr. Baswell that he didn't know how high they went up in the air, but that he came down easy. The others were blown away and killed.]

There was a fellow down there by the name of Bill Black who peddled sewing machines. And he had an old horse and a little old buggy with a place in the back, you know, where he put a machine for a sample. And this old horse was grazing in his backyard. Well, it blowed it all away, you

An old-style storm cellar on Chickalah Mountain. Except for this cellar, every trace of the house that stood on this spot is gone.

A "new-style" storm cellar on Chickalah Mountain.

see, and they didn't know where the horse or anybody else
was. But, you know, they found that horse about a mile up
there in a man's lot, a-pickin' grass. It picked him up,
carried him over there, and set him down in that fellow's
lot; and didn't hurt him a bit. [All of these are common
occurrences in tornadoes.]

Then Mr. Baswell told some of his own experiences on
the day of the storm:

We could see it coming—we was used to it in them days.
We all went over to my neighbor Casey's because he had a
basement and we thought we'd all be safe in there. I went
out on his front porch and I looked and I saw a thing
comin' off the mountain. Up there like a ball of fire! And I
said, "Chester, come here quick," and he come out there
and he saw that thing coming, and he said, "For God's sake,
let's get in the basement." All run in, you know.

Well, it come and blowed his top (roof) away, you know,
and his house went about six or eight inches off the
foundation. We was all in the cellar. It got dark and blowed
all the windows out and the doors open down in that
basement, and our hair was matted with that mud.

Later, when it was all over, Mr. Baswell said, "Me and
my neighbor built us a storm cellar right on the line, and
when they predict a tornado we go down in there. We
don't take any chances."

Another survivor, Almeda Riddle, had a more tragic
experience:

We had been to a Thanksgiving dinner. The factory for
which my husband worked had given a dinner and all of
the staff and the hands were invited. And we had just
gotten back home and I had pulled my glasses off and layed
them aside, thankfully that I did because they were glass
glasses back fifty years ago. I washed my face and looked
out across the back of the house and called my husband to
come and look at this cloud. And he looked and he said,
"That's a tornado"; and I said, "Well, let's get to the storm

Almeda Riddle sits on the stile at her parents' home place, near the town of Heber Springs.

house. Remember this thing's been blown away three times." And he said, "I don't believe we have time."

We ran in the neighbor's house—they were all on the same lot. And when we went in there to get the keys—just about the time we got into the house—it went! The last thing I remember of my husband—the last act that he did—it was hailing and the wind was blowing when we went in until I had to crawl up the steps with my baby. When we got in I said, "They're already gone. They've left a light burning." And "Let's go." And he shook his head. There was a big rock chimney—an old-fashioned fireplace—and this house was built of *heavy* timbers. And he pushed us into the corner of the house and put his arms, like that, around the four children and me and that's the last thing I remembered. I saw that side of the house come up—I saw it lift. I screamed, and that's the last thing I remember.

After the tornado was over she came to and she recalled: "When the lightning would flash I could see and I looked out toward town and I could see it was just in a blaze. Of course our house burned—it blew away but it burned also."

I asked her, "From the lightning?" and she replied, "No. People left these oil lamps burning and fires in open fireplaces and wood stoves burning."

Her brother-in-law and the man who owned the house came and took them to the storm cellar. Her husband and the baby she held in her arms were killed. Almeda's hip was broken, one child was scalped, and another child's leg was crushed.

On another day she told this story about the storm:

I never open a jar of apple jelly that is clear and red and beautiful that I don't think of my husband, even though it's been over forty-five years since his death. On that Thanksgiving morning we had just finished breakfast and the family had eaten up the last of a jar of apple jelly. My husband was sitting at the breakfast table holding our baby, we called him C.C., and he started pestering me to open up another jar of apple jelly.

I told him I wasn't a-gonna do it because there was just one jar left and if I opened it there wouldn't be any left for Christmas. He kept on and on a-pestering and finally he started bouncing C.C. on his knee saying, "C.C., tell your mama that she'll have apple jelly for the rest of her life, but she may not always have you and me." I told 'em they were just trying to play on my sympathies and I didn't have a bit of sympathy for either one of 'em; but I got busy and fixed them some more hot biscuits and opened that jar of apple jelly. I can still see them sitting there enjoying it and the way that baby's face looked so happy over that apple jelly. Right after that the tornado came and took them away from me and I have been so glad that the rest of my life I haven't had to live knowing that I hadn't opened that jar of apple jelly.

After these tragic events, Almeda's father and a neighbor, Ruby Dylan, wrote this ballad, which they entitled:

THE STORM OF HEBER SPRINGS, NOVEMBER 25th, 1926

'Twas on Thanksgiving Day
The town of Heber Springs
Was visited by a cyclone
And partly swept away.

The people no doubt were feasting
And never thought so soon
That by a dreadful cyclone
They'd shortly meet their doom.

They saw the storm approaching
The clouds looked low and black,
And through that little city,
It left a dreadful track.

They saw the cyclone coming,
And it's too sad to relate
The happiest of families
That had to separate.

They saw the lightning flashing;
They heard the thunder roar.
Such tears were in that city
Was never known before.

And as the storm came near them,
They heard the people cry:
"O Lord, have mercy on us!
Is this our time to die?"

Some people in that city
Declared it was God's wrath,
To course the great tornado
To take them in its path.

They pointed to their churches
Where they'd refused to go
To pay to their Redeemer
The debt of love they owed.

This ballad points out the fact that the churches bore the
brunt of the storm. As Mr. Baswell said, the brick walls of
the churches just fell outward, not toward the inside, and
the Methodist Church and the Baptist Church both blew
away. This was typical in a tornado and led to the folk
belief that God was punishing the people for not attending
church more often. However, according to scientists much
of the wreckage in a tornado is caused by explosion, and
any building with its windows and doors tightly closed
would blow itself to pieces. In fact, the *Arkansas Gazette*
reported that:

A riddle that plagued the Midwestern states for years
was the fact that in any town where a tornado struck, the

church was usually the first building to go, while the saloons invariably survived. It came to be a sore spot with religious folk that was finally eased when modern weathermen pointed out that the church, closed all week, made an ideal target, while the saloon, with swinging half doors in constant use, was able to withstand.

Today cyclone cellars are still built beside homes lying in the storm belt (also called "tornado lane" and "cyclone alley") and many owners use them whenever a storm threatens. On a dark and windy day if you go to a country home and find no one there, try the storm shelter before you leave. You may find the people (especially old folks) waiting inside until the storm blows over, since they remember other storms and stories of other storms and feel it's safest to go to the cellar "jest in case!"

THE CORNCRIB, THE BARN, AND THE COTTONSEED HOUSE

Once the farmer had his fields fenced he got out his mule and began to plow. In the early days one of his principal crops was corn, and even today most farmhouses have a corn patch in the side yard, or in the back lot, or mixed in with the zinnia bed.

This versatile food was eaten morning, noon, and night. It was cooked on the cob as "roasting ears," cut off the cob to make hominy, and ground up to make cornmeal. The stalks made fodder for the animals and the cobs became dolls, pipes, jelly, and torches. The shucks were cut into strips to make shoelaces, mattresses, and brooms; plaited to make horse collars and hats; woven to make chair seats; and studied carefully by the farmer when he was forecasting the weather. All in all there is probably as much folklife tied up in the cornstalk as in any other one thing.

When the corn was harvested it was often stored in a

corncrib. In Arkansas it was customary for the corn to be stored with the shuck still on and the shuck to be taken off as the corn was used. However, according to Aunt Chat, corn huskings were held "once in a great while." She told how "They'd shuck the corn out of one crib, you see, and put it in another. They had to carry it when they'd have corn huskings. They'd make a party out of it—that's what the fun was. Everybody'd come and shuck corn." Farmer Wilhite said that the boy who found a "red ear of corn, or any different from the usual white or yellow, he got to kiss his girl."

In addition to shucking corn they sometimes pulled fodder. This was done in July or August before the stalk was dead. Aunt Chat recalled how "They'd pull the fodder off the stalk by the handful and then they'd take two or three blades and wrap around and tie it. That made a *hand.* You broke the stalk over and put that fodder on top of it. And when you got it all pulled you'd tie four hands together and that'd make a *bundle.* That bundle was enough for a horse."*

The fodder was stored in the barn. This was usually the largest of the outbuildings and was often built with the help of the neighbors, just as the cabin had been. When a log-rolling was held to clear the new land a barn was built with some of the logs. Two ladies at the Willow House told me they remembered attending barn-raisings as recently as thirty-five years ago, and explained: "They'd have log-rollings. That was when they was building a barn for someone. The women would quilt and the men would all get together and go out in the woods and cut the logs and come in and build the barn. And the women would bring the food and serve the lunch and quilt."

In addition to corn, cotton was raised all over Arkansas

---

*When she grew tobacco, Aunt Chat said, "I pulled the tobacco, and 'handed' it up and dried it. There was an old couple and they chewed up most of it. They'd pay so much a hand." She also said you didn't pull fodder until "after the dew begin to fall" (in the evening).

Because there was no corn in Europe before the discovery of America, the corncrib is truly American. A corncrib in Newton County "right handy" to the corn.

The Rainbolts' corncrib in Stone County.

at one time. As Roy Simpson said, "The chief cash crop of the farmers was cotton, and the chief feed crop was corn." Mrs. Joyce agreed that "A farmer's sole means of making money was cotton." She told how tenant farmers rented land on "the third and the fourth." This meant that the tenant gave the landlord a third of the corn he raised (measured in wagonloads) and a fourth of the cotton (measured in bales). She recalled that one of their outbuildings was a cottonseed house. When they went to milk the cows at night they always stopped by the cottonseed house to get a bucket of cottonseeds to give the cows. This kept the cows quiet while they were being milked.

These three buildings (plus their friend—the chicken house) make an excellent study of the changes and contrasts in mountain life. The corncrib has become an occasional building. Certainly there is not one behind every farmhouse but they are easy to find.

A barn often had a place to park the wagon. This is a typical barn in the Ouachita Mountains.

The barn has remained constant. Because *log* barns are still being built by thrifty farmers they are much easier to find than log cabins. Also, a farmer is less likely to "upgrade" his barn by covering it with planks or tarpaper. For this reason there are barns all over the state with notched log walls, shingled roofs, and handmade latches on the doors. They come in all styles—single, double, one-story, and two-story—and an observant traveler should have no trouble finding one while driving on almost any dirt road.

Today, the cottonseed house is gone from the mountains. The land of the mountains was poor land for cotton farming, and in this century farmers switched over to raising chickens and cattle. The henhouse stands where the cottonseed house once stood and even here the times are changing.

All over the northern part of the state there are enormous broiler houses where the food, water, temperature, and the entire life of the chickens is electronically controlled. Only occasionally do you find someone like Paty who has a little log chicken house that she and her husband built many years ago. Inside she has a woodburning stove that she lights every spring. Then she sprinkles sand on the floor, gets a new batch of baby chicks, and declares: "Those are the happiest chicks you ever seen." In addition, she has a shelf for drying her sweet potatoes inside the henhouse.

THE ASH HOPPER AND THE WASHPOT

When the wild flowers began coming up in the creek bottoms and the moon was in the right sign, it was time for making lye soap. Behind each cabin was an ash hopper, located (as one woman remembered) "right in the middle of our play space when we were kids." Roxie Dooley recalled how her mother and other pioneer women dumped all their fireplace ashes in the big V-shaped hopper all through the winter. By spring the ashes were rotten and ready for soap-making.

Most people preferred hardwood ashes, for as Fred High said, "The lye was not good if the wood that was burnt for it was not good. My mother would taste the ashes to see if they was good to make soap with. Sometimes she would keep the ashes two years or more, as they would be like whiskey—it is said when old it is better."

When the day came for making the soap, the men and boys would take the top off the hopper and make furrows in the ashes with a hoe. Buckets of water were poured over the ashes until pure lye ran out the hollow-log trough underneath. This yellow lye would run down into the drip pan at the base of the trough.

Meanwhile the women were cooking all the leftover scraps of fat meat, stale grease, and sometimes even bones, in a big iron kettle. When the men went possum or coon hunting they'd skin the animal for its hide and give the meat to their wives for the soap kettle. Occasionally even the better meat went in, for as Farmer Wilhite explained:

It's a funny thing to me how they'd eat the old fatback and other stuff and save these hams, shoulders, and things, you know, for a special occasion. Well, any meat cured with the bone in it is hard to keep, and the next thing you know there'd come a warm spell and these'd spoil. Well, there was the hams then that went into the soap barrel instead of on the table.

After the lye and the lard were both ready they were mixed together in the big iron kettle and cooked until the mixture was thick. While it was cooking it was stirred with the battlin' stick.*

*This was the long paddle used to beat the clothes clean on washday. My father-in-law remembered, "We used to soak the old dirty overalls—soak 'em overnight—and then put 'em on a stump, or have a block; and have a paddle and knock some of that dirt out. They'd be clean but it'd wear 'em out pretty much." Annie Campbell called this the "punchin' stick"; and Aunt Willie recalled an old play-party game called All Around the Old Soapsticks.

An ash hopper in Stone County.

*Mr. Wittenberg makes lye soap
"thick as thickenin' gravy."*

Mr. E. L. Wittenberg, who still makes lye soap in an old iron kettle, said it should be cooked "until it is about as thick as thickenin' gravy. When it looks good enough to eat it's ready to pour up." If the soap was taken up while it was still jellylike, it was called soft soap; hence the expression, "Don't let 'em soft soap you." The thicker soap was poured into a pan where it was allowed to cool and then was cut into squares. Patience poured her "cold water lye soap" into empty matchboxes to give it a neat, rectangular, "store-bought" shape. Some people let their soap rest for six weeks before using it; since, as one man claimed, "fresh-made soap takes the skin off'n yor hands."

Everyone agreed that lye soap would eat up everything except the inside of the old iron pot it was made in. It was used as a sure cure for skin diseases such as impetigo; for cleaning floors, clothes, kids, and all-comers; and one man even used it as part of his secret fish bait formula. It was considered fatal if eaten, but Brother Lonzo Tallent told about the time his mother's soft soap ended up as dog food:

> Me and my brother had us a hound apiece, and they probably needed feedin' a whole lot oftener than they got it. But they's hungry enough anyway! And she set a bucket of lye soap down out there, and that dog ran and got in and just went to drinkin' it—the fresh soap. And we counted him a dead dog—but he just got fat!

Today there are still many people who make their own lye soap, on the theory that nothing else will clean as well. People gave me tan soap, white soap, and soft soap. They also gave me their favorite folk beliefs (some of them contradictory) on making soap:

To get nice light soap you make it in the light of the moon.

Soap won't thicken unless it's made in the dark of the moon.

It won't thicken anyway "if stirred by a lazy person."

Only one person should stir the soap—never different people.

But no matter what their advice, they all echoed Bill Blevin's warning to be careful or "It'll take the hide off'n ye."

THE BEE YARD

> Marriage, birth or buryin'
> News across the seas,
> All your sad or merryin'
> You must tell the bees.
> (Rudyard Kipling, "The Bee-boy's Song")

It has been said that people go from the necessities of life to the pleasures; and the pioneer was no exception. After he had surrounded his home with all the necessary structures, he usually added some bee gums to be sure and have the pleasure of some "sweetenin'."

Tracing the bees was a favorite sport in the early days and for most men it was usually combined with hunting, fishing, clearing the land, or any other outside activity. However, dedicated bee hunters would neglect all their other business to hunt the bees in the spring of the year. And like all hunters they had their favorite tall tales, such as this one by Farmer Wilhite:

> There was a story 'bout one feller. The bees swarmed and the only thing he had around there was a five-gallon keg. So he caught the swarm in that five-gallon keg. And it was a good year for flowers and stuff that way; and he got ten gallons of strained honey outta that five-gallon keg.

Since bee hunting is still done in the same ways throughout Arkansas, many people gave their ideas, superstitions, and suggestions on the subject of bees. Most of the ideas on the subject had been handed down

A bee yard in Pulaski County.

through many generations and it was amazing to see how similar the techniques were, even in greatly separated areas.

Everyone agreed that the first step in bee tracing was finding the bees, and there were several ways to do this. Jim Bixler said, "I'd course 'em off of flowers in the spring of the year. I'd find 'em on flowers or water." In dry weather bees would go to the ponds or any standing water and the hunter could find them there. Newman said that on Chickalah Mountain, where there were no ponds, people could hardly water the horses in the summer because the bees would be so thick at the horses' buckets; and Roy Simpson said you could usually find them around the outdoor toilets.

If a hunter couldn't locate them at a water or a flower source he could always bait the bees. To do this most people put out a mixture of sweetenin' and water or a piece of the honeycomb with' some of the honey still in it.

At the other extreme, Roy Simpson said, "The love of the bee for urine led to the use of 'stink bait.' In our area it normally consisted of cobs soaked with urine, although something other than cobs could be used." The bait was placed in a dish and put on an old stump standing out in a field. Sometimes the hunter would soak a corncob in the bait and place it on the stump; and in Montgomery County bee hunters would fill their mouths with the sweetened water and spit it out, spraying it all over the bushes.

Once the bait was out, the hunter would wait patiently until a bee came to the spot he had staked out and then he would follow the bee back to its hive. After the bee had sweetenin' it always made a direct, perfectly straight line for its home. The path these bees took was called a "course" and following it was known as "coursing the bees." In the early days honey was so valued that the knowledge of a bee course was used as an object of trade; and Kermit said he could remember his Uncle Johnny Moody trading a plowhead to a man for a calf and two bee courses.

An old woman who had worked with bees all her life told me that once inside the hive the bees do a dance to show the other bees where the bait is. They zigzag their bodies and turn them at a certain angle to the sun, which tells the other bees where to go. Soon a steady line of bees will be set up. Dr. Olen Nail explained a similar idea: "When a working bee discovers a good nectar flow, she returns to the hive and executes the 'honey run.' She runs a given distance in a certain direction, thus telling the other bees the direction and distance of the nectar flow."

After the bee has its bait it will usually circle several times to get some height before it makes its beeline for home. Walter Yardley remembered being with his uncle one time when a bee would come, take their bait, and then circle so many times that they would lose him. Finally, the old man decided to physically follow the bee as it circled. As he ran around and around the stump, following the bee, he got so dizzy he fell over the stump and almost killed himself.

This was either a common occurrence, or a popular story, because Roland Gillihan told an almost identical tale:

> Old Uncle Cagle Canard and Jodie Burns—they bee hunted together all the time. And Uncle Cagle had a new-ground field,* and they's stumps in that field, and he had a bee course there. And he kept follerin' these bees and he never could find 'em. So he got Jodie out there and he says, "Jodie," says, "you get here where they're feedin' and I'll get out yonder aways, and when one starts you tell me." And directly Jodie said, "Cagle, he's a-comin'." And Cagle, when he seen him, he put his finger up and just kept pointin' as he went along, and turned and was just headin' as hard as he could a-watchin' him, and he run over a stump and he liked to killed himself. Just like to killed him, shor 'nuff, and there ain't no joke about that.

After they located the hives there were various ways of collecting the honey, or the bees, or both. If they were just after the honey they could simply rob the hive. If they wanted a permanent hive they could take their own bee box and capture the queen and the other bees would follow. To do this Farmer said they would "get a bee gum all fixed up and beat on a pan by the hive and the bees would go in it." Jim said the noise causes the bees to settle, and he told this story:

> After my great-grandfather was old, he tended bees. He had a large orchard and he had a hive of bees settin' by practically ever tree. He'd lay out there in the spring of the year on a sheep's hide watchin' for 'em to swarm. When they'd swarm, why, he'd holler for his wife Peggy and his daughter Allie and they'd come out and beat on the pans and make all the noise they could—even ring the dinner bell. Try to get 'em to settle. He'd hive 'em then—put 'em in the hives.

*A "new-ground" field is a field that has just been cleared.

Usually the hunter cut the tree at the base and again over the top of the hive and brought that section home with him. One of the favorite trees that bees choose for their hives is a hollow gum tree and for that reason these sections of trees were known in the early days as bee gums. Later, when the men began building boxes for their hives, they still called them bee gums, or (to indicate the new style of gums) "patented gums."

If a hunter discovered a bee tree but couldn't cut it that day he made his mark on the tree to show that it was his; and came back to cut it later. Jim told how "Once you find a tree you're supposed to mark it, you know. You just put a cross on it. The owner of the tree—if he's not willin', why you ain't allowed to cut it and he's not either. If you can get the bees out without harmin' the tree why he can't keep you from it. Most of 'em'll let you cut it unless it's a witness tree* or a shade tree in the yard or something like that."

The next logical question in bee hunting is, Why don't the hunters get stung? The answer is that they often do—supposedly women less often than men. One woman explained, "If you are gentle with the bees they'll be gentle with you; if you're savage with the bees they'll be savage with you." One man said you should work with bees on a sunny day because in stormy weather they have a bad disposition. Almost all agreed: "Bees knows when you're afraid same as a dog or a snake knows when you're afraid."

Most hunters wore a veil and used some sort of smoking device to keep the bees away from them. They made or bought a "smoker," which was a bucket-type tin can with a spout. Inside it they burned rags, hickory chips, dry grass,

---

*Another "folk tree" was the witness tree. Guy Smith defined a witness tree: "This was usually a tree that was close to the corner of the survey. They'd skin the bark off of it and put an identification mark there of the location of that corner. They just cut off a small portion of the bark and they'd put the number of the quarter section on there." Jim Bixler added, "That'd grow back over sometimes and I've seen 'em come back later and take an ax and chop a big chip outta there—and there would be the number in there."

Colonel Buxton explained how the numbers were cut: "You use a scribe awl. It cuts a little trench in the tree. You chop the bark off and write right on the tree with a scribing awl. It is put on the side of the tree facing the corner. They have one witness tree at each one of the four quarter sections."

Bill Blevins said, "This old tree is full of honey, but I can't cut it down, 'cause it's my witness tree."

or anything that would smoke but not flame. Instead of a smoker others burned pine knots or made the rags into a ball and put it on the end of a stick. Tom Patrick said he "rolled up rags 'bout the size of your arm and set it afire. Then I blowed the smoke in." Just the right amount of smoke would cause the bees to go to their cells and remain there eating honey. Some people even gave the bees a whiff of tobacco to make them drunk and docile.

Besides bee stings and falling over stumps there were other hazards a hunter could encounter. For example, Tom told this story:

> One time me and my daddy went out and we had a bee course—we watched 'em water and go to a tree. And we got to the tree and we couldn't see no bees. And Pa said to me, he said, "I believe I seen a bee go down the tree." He says, "Now, son, they go in a hole at the top and go down in the tree." And he got up on a nearby treetop that had been cut—to see—and he got to rockin'—and he fell down on a rattlesnake that had twenty-five rattles and a button!* He got off of it 'fore it bit him, and got outta there—and didn't go back till the snake got away. But we got thirty or forty pounds out of that arm.

(This has to rank as another tall tale since it's hard to believe anyone counted twenty-five rattles on a snake that got away!)

Other tips on dealing with bees were:

1. Wool cloth should never be burned around bees. Some said wool smoke would make the bees attack while others said it would kill them. Supposedly the bees prefer cotton to wool because cotton comes from plants, which bees like, and wool comes from animals, which they don't like.

2. The type of flower determines the type of honey. For example, black-locust flowers make a darker honey than clover does. Bob Blair said that sometimes men would put their hives in the backs of their trucks and take them down to a clover field that was in bloom or to a black-locust thicket, and leave them to get the kind of honey they preferred. Newman said that on the mountain the farmers used to sow buckwheat just for the bees to have to make honey.

Jim Bixler felt that "What they start workin' on they'll work on that flower as long as they can get it. The older

*A button is a rattle that hasn't completely formed.

the flowers get the stronger they get, you see, and that's where you get your darkest honey. It's heavier and you get more minerals in it—it's better for medical purpose."

3. Never wear black, especially a black hat, around bees. Black makes them angry.

4. The best time to hunt for bees is in the early spring. Jim said you should cut the tree "along in May or June to save the bees." Fred High quoted an old saying:

> A swarm of bees in May
> Is worth a stack of hay,
> A swarm of bees in June
> Is worth a silver spoon,
> And a swarm in July
> Is worth a green fly. (Worthless)

This same saying, in a slightly different form, is known in England, where it goes:

> A swarm of bees in May
> Is worth a load of hay.
> A swarm of bees in June
> Is worth a silver spoon.
> A swarm of bees in July
> Is not worth a fly.

Like many other groups, bee hunters have their own vocabulary. In addition to "coursing the bees," "patented gums," and the "honey run," they used several other terms, such as:

"Cornering the bees"—Some hunters set their bait and keep moving it along about 300 yards in the right direction every time the bee comes back. Jim said he would take a pan of honey as bait and move it along until he had the beeline located. Then if he still couldn't find the tree, "You go way over to one side, you see, maybe a quarter of a mile, and you put it out over there. And they come right back [to the bait] and cross your line and that's what you call 'gettin' 'em cornered.' When you get 'em cornered and still can't find 'em that's when the old-timers say, 'You lose a crop then.'"

Newman told about another tracing technique called "timing the bees." A really experienced bee hunter would stay by the bait, time the bee until it returned, and then estimate how far away the hive was. Since he knew the direction by watching the bee take off he could usually walk right to it.

"Honey flow"—This is the time when the bees are able to get nectar from the flowers. A hard rain or the end of the season for a certain flower will end that honey flow and then the bees will cap their honey.

"Capping"—The bees cap the honey or seal it over after they cure it.

"Curing"—According to Jim the bees fan 50 percent of the moisture out of the honey by beating their wings and "fanning it out." "They keep that air stirring in there all time. It has to be cured or it'll make you sick."

"Blaze 'em out"—Jim said: "I have seen it when they [the bees] went a good ways, you know, or went around the hillside. Then you blaze 'em out. Take two men—he'd go on over there and you'd keep in a straight line." When they finally got to the spot it took good eyes to locate them because, as Farmer said, "Bees go in and out a mighty little hole like a peckerwood hole or under a knothole." Jim told how he had "found 'em goin' in at the ground; I've found 'em in logs; I've found 'em in a bluff of rock—you know, along the creek."

Once the bees were safely home they were a source of honey for many years. Often they became almost human to the people who worked with them, and the custom of "telling the bees" (when there was a death in the family, etc.) came over from England with the earliest pioneers. Dr. Nail explained this custom as he learned it from Vaughn and Paul Wilson, beekeeping brothers of Batesville and Lake City.

Legend has it that in case a beekeeper dies, his bees will languish and eventually die. Someone in the family goes and talks to the bees and tells them their master has passed away, that they are getting a new master who will take good care of them. They are not to worry, their new master will do as well by them as their old master. They are to work for this new master as diligently as they did for their old master. Then, someone in the family takes over the bees or they are sold or given away. Legend says that after the talk, the bees will do well.

The pioneers used the honey for everything from sweetenin' in sassafras tea to making cough syrup (when mixed with a little whiskey). The beeswax was rolled out to make candles; and both honey and beeswax were a valuable cash crop. For these reasons the bee gums added the final touch of enjoyment to all the outbuildings of the pioneer homestead.

Postscript—Where Have All the Wild Bees Gone?

In 1972 a headline in the *Arkansas Gazette* said, STATE'S FARMERS KILLING FRIENDS, THE HONEYBEES. The article pointed out the fact that Arkansas is killing its bees through pesticide poisoning, and in doing so is heading for "an agricultural disaster." Not only are the people who raise the bees as a business being hurt by this, but cattle farmers and other farmers who rely on the bees for pollination of their plants and pasture grasses are suffering. It has become necessary to move beehives around the state to pollinate orchards and vegetable gardens.

There are ways to prevent this, such as spraying late in the day and notifying the beekeepers before spraying begins. However, according to the article, "there are no state or federal laws governing the use of pesticides in

relation to the welfare of honeybees and their keepers."
Truly this state, and other agricultural states, will suffer as
the honeybees begin to disappear.

Newman expressed the problem when he said, "Used to,
up until just a few years ago, ever time a flower or
anything opened here there was just bees all over the
place. But I haven't seen a bee now in I don't know how
long. This insecticide that they used has killed off most of
'em, you see." Or as Farmer Wilhite put it, "The bees as
well as the bugs are being eliminated, simply because this
poison don't know the difference between a bee and a
bug."

An empty bee gum.

The old farm wagon.

Going to town—the old ways meet the new.

CHAPTER 4
TOWN LIFE

As the farms grew closer and closer together small towns began to develop. At first these were not very big; in fact, Gerstaeker found the county seat of Perry County—"two houses and a stable." Before long, however, most small towns could boast of a mill, a general store, a blacksmith shop, a school, at least one church, and sometimes a saloon. All of these were gathering places in the early days and many of them still serve that purpose today.

THE BLACKSMITH SHOP

The blacksmith was the original handyman. He made and repaired the farm implements for the farmer, made new shoes for the farmer's horses, made kitchen utensils for the farmer's wife; and even made the tools for his own trade. As Warren Wilhite said, "A community could get along without a doctor better than they could without a blacksmith."

One of the most interesting traditions associated with the blacksmith shop was the ancient custom of firing the

An old log blacksmith shop in the Ozarks.

anvil. It has often been said that the mountain people of
Arkansas are "twice-a-mountaineers," since most of the
early settlers came from the eastern mountains. With them
they brought their old customs that had been derived
from even earlier traditions in the British Isles. One of
these was the habit of gathering at the smith for a shooting
of the anvil on festive occasions.

In *Discovering Folklore in Industry*, Alan Smith writes that
in England, "The blacksmith's traditional mode of
celebration was exploding gunpowder on their anvils. This
was done for weddings but most often on November 23rd,
the feast of St. Clement, the patron saint of blacksmiths."
In Arkansas the custom was practiced not only for
marriages, but at Christmas, New Year's, the Fourth of
July, and (if the blacksmith's candidate won), on election

night. In fact it was reported that in a Boone County election of 1873 "free watermelons provided the votes and an anvil was fired to celebrate the victory." A blacksmith in Stone County told me that he only fired the anvil in the middle of the night on Christmas Eve and they called it the "Christmas Gun."

Most of the old blacksmiths have fired the anvil at some time and they all agree on how it was done, with very few variations. According to Jim Dan Powell, a blacksmith in the Ozarks, "You put one anvil down bottom up. . . . You fill this hole that's in the anvil bottom with the powder and you set this other anvil right over that hole. And you put a little powder out here, you know, where it come out to the edge, and then you took a stick or something with fire on it and tetched it off. It'd knock that anvil as high as this ceiling. See, that holds you a handful of powder almost. And it's pretty well confined in those holes, you know."

Elmer Moody said they "put the other anvil on it with a

The blacksmith's anvil.

fuse coming out the side. Then you set the fuse off and run." Bob Blair recalled how they always used black powder because it was slower burning. In the Ouachita Mountains, Farmer Wilhite said they would "pour about a teacup of powder in that hole and then string some powder out to one side to light it by. Then they'd slip the top anvil over the hole. They'd take a fishing gig* and heat it till it is red-hot and then everybody gets back, and boy, you'd *better* get back! And they'd stick that red-hot iron to that powder. Well, it flashes over to the middle and boom it goes. I've seen those anvils go twelve or fifteen feet high. Course if it's pretty well balanced over the hole it'll go straight up, but if it isn't balanced over the hole it'll go sideways and then you'd better look out. Cause you take a hundred pound anvil coming from up in the air, why, you don't wanta butt heads with it."

The explosion could be heard for miles around. Sim Goodman recalled, "When Teddy Roosevelt was elected President, Tom Ashcraft and Virg Ashcraft [the local Republicans] got old Uncle Eppes Billingsley's anvils and fired 'em right here on the court square. They loaded those things up and I mean they sounded like there was a war going on." Mr. Hardgrave told how they got just as much noise with only one anvil:

---

*Gigs were also made by the blacksmith. Roy Simpson said they "were made of iron, shaped like a trident, and attached to a long handle." Gigging was a nighttime sport and Mr. Simpson explained how it was done: "The boat was lighted by a pine knot fire. Our boats, ordinarily built of pine, had seats in the middle and at the back. In gigging nobody sat. The giggers stood up, poling the boat with the inverted gig, until a fish was sighted. This was possible because gigging was done in fairly shallow water. For light, the center seat was covered deeply with mud to form a place where the fire could burn without damage to the boat. One gigger stood behind the fire and the other in front."

In his book, Stars Upstream, Leonard Hall told the story about some fishermen in the hills who had a jug of mountain dew that they were enjoying while they were out gigging. They also had a big pile of pine knots which caught fire and caught the boat on fire. When the gigger in the stern realized what had happened he shouted, "Hey, boys, the boat's afire! Pole for Gravel Spring." Then, according to Mr. Hall, "At this moment his long-shafted gig caught under a rock in the river bottom and jerked him overboard. As he came sputtering up, an idea struck him. 'Never mind poling for Gravel Spring, boys,' he shouted. 'Here's water.'"

We always just used a rock—a big, flat rock. And filled this anvil full of powder—you know it's hollow up in there. We had to turn it upside down to load it and we'd have a fuse to go into that. We generally had 'em about that far [several feet] so it'd give you plenty of time to get away. You'd put it on that big rock and light that fuse—and when it went off it'd sound, oh, kinda like a cannon. They'd do that generally the last night of the old year.*

Today there are very few blacksmith shops, and firecrackers have taken the place of anvil firings. This is less noisy and less dangerous, perhaps, but not as exciting. After he described the way to fire an anvil, Jim Dan Powell looked sad as he said, "They used to do that a lotta times along about Christmas and on the Fourth of July. But they don't do that anymore of late years."

SCHOOLS

Briar, wire, limber lock,
Three geese in a flock.
One flew east,
One flew west,
One flew over the cuckoo's nest.
O-U-T spells out.
Be gone your long way home.
(Old Schoolyard Chant—Remembered by
Aunt Willie)

*The ceremony of "Shooting the New Year In" is one of the holiday rituals that has made the transition from the old country to Appalachia to the Ozarks, with some changes along the way. In The Golden Bough, Sir James Frazer discusses the public expulsion of evils as an ancient custom and says, "On New Year's Eve, which is Saint Sylvester's Day, Bohemian lads, armed with guns, form themselves into circles and fire thrice into the air. This is called 'Shooting the Witches' and is supposed to frighten the witches away." In a 1774 diary entry the Reverend Ludolf Bachhof of North Carolina told how he could get no rest on New Year's Eve because a crowd of young men were going about from farm to farm "'shooting in' the year." He went on to say that he heard the shooting until sunrise, and "one might have thought the whole neighborhood was full of Indians. All who came to the noon meeting had much to say about what a noisy night it was, and how they had been disturbed." In the Ozarks the houses were too scattered and the hills were too steep for boys to go from house to house. But a gathering at the blacksmith shop to fire the anvil made enough noise for all the people and all the witches to hear.

The earliest schools were informal and irregular affairs. Even in this century some of the mountain schools were of the "farm-rhythm" type and lasted only through the eighth grade. Since many of the teachers were also farmers, and most of the students had to help their families in the fields, a term of school was rarely ever held during the planting or harvesting season. As Fred High explained, "When I was old enough to learn I was big enough to work and I had to do that"; but Aunt Edna remembered that at Box Springs (where she taught) "When the crops were laid by,* the big boys who had finished eighth grade would come back to school because they didn't have anything else to do." Because of this, many of the country students were older and bigger than their teacher.

One of the earliest schools in the state was the one at Little Piney taught by Albert Pike, who received his pay half in cash and half in pigs. To get this school, Pike (who was later governor of Arkansas) asked one of the mountaineers about his prospects, and received this answer:

"Why," said he, "if you would set in, right straight, I reckon thar' might be a right smart chance of scholars got, as we have had no teacher here for the best end of two years. Thar's about fifteen families on the creek, and the whole tote of 'em well fixed for children. They want a schoolmaster pretty much, too. We got a teacher about six months ago—a Scotchman, or an Irishman, I think. He took up for six months, and carried his proposals around, and he got twenty scholars directly. It weren't long, though, before he cut up some ferlicues, and got into a priminary; and so one morning he was found among the missing."

---

*"Laying by" was the time when the cultivation of the crops ceased. This season usually started in early July, after the spring planting and early cultivation was over; and lasted until fall, when the harvest began.

The log school on Weather's Mountain.

When Pike asked how he was to get the school the old man answered:

> "I'll tell you. You must make out your proposals to take up school; tell them how much you ask a month, and what you can teach; and write it out as fine as you can, I reckon you're a pretty good scribe, and in the morning there's to be a shooting match here for beef; nearly all the settlement will be here, and you'll get signers enough."

In any area, as soon as there were enough people to form a settlement, the men got together and built a log schoolhouse. The school was used as a church when a preacher came around, as a voting place on election day, and as a meeting place whenever there was a special occasion. For many years the only Christmas tree in each community was the one at the school.

The life of a country schoolteacher was not an easy one. Aunt Willie recalled the time she left home (at the age of fifteen) to go across the mountain to teach her first school:

Sunday, the journey was made by hack over almost impassable roads. It was strictly a sharecropping area. I was to board at the only house with two fireplaces; and share the room with three little ones. The family consisted of an elderly couple, two widowers, one bachelor, and six grandchildren from nine to eighteen. When my father drove away I thought I would choke.

About dark the old grandmother came in, squatted down by the fire, and gave a few mournful sighs. Then she said, "I don't know what we can have for supper." I assured her I couldn't eat a bite. Finally she said, "Well, I reckon we could have some roasted turnips." In spite of my pleadings the turnips were brought in, roasted in the ashes, and eaten with relish.

At five o'clock the next morning I went to breakfast. There I met the old gentleman who was not only lord and master of his household, but was president, secretary, and treasurer of the school board. He informed me that he had the rules and regulations ready for me to read each Monday morning. I hurried to school to build a fire and sweep the floor. At eight o'clock I rang the bell, though the three little children were already seated quietly. I was handed two pages of foolscap paper from which I read.

When left alone I took stock. The building was located behind a high hill, with no other building in sight. A dim road led to it but none passed by. The front doors were securely barred. There were a few benches, a blackboard, two first readers, one second reader, and my own story and poem books. We memorized, pantomimed, and dramatized poems and stories in many different versions. Acorns and hickory nuts were used for number games.

After the scattern cotton was picked the enrollment boomed to twenty. There was never a dull moment. We worked, studied, sang, and played together.

Today schoolchildren still play a few of the old-time games, but most of the old favorites have almost disappeared. Here are three slightly different versions of one that was popular with the girls:

CHICKAMY, CHICKAMY, CRANEY CROW*

(Granny Riddle's version)

You have them all lined up and the Old Hen stands at the head of the line. The Old Hen says this:

Chickamy, chickamy, cranny 'ma crow,
Went to the well to wash his toe;
And got back and my little black-eyed chicken was gone.
What time is it, Old Witch?

One of the little chickens goes out and the other children stay. You go on until all the children that are the chickens are gone.

(Aunt Willie's version)

Chick an a chick an a cranny crow,
I went to the well to wash my toe.
When I got back my chicks were gone.
What time a day is it, Old Witch?

---

*In Georgia this game was called Chicken, Chicken, Crane or Crow?—which makes more sense.

Sometimes there is a group of nonsense questions which follow, such as:

> [Witch] What'd you come after?
>
> [Child] Come after some fire.
>
> [Witch] I got no fire.
>
> [Child] Well, I thought I seen smoke coming out of your chimney.
>
> [Witch] No, that was the children playing in the ashes.
>
> [Child] Well, what time is it, Old Witch?
>
> [Witch] Time for you to go home.
>
> [Child] Can I get home by candlelight?
>
> [Witch] Yes, if your legs are long and light.

In some versions, when they ask what time it is everyone counts to twelve. At this, all the children scatter and hide until the old witch catches them.

This same game was played by the little black girls, as told to me by my friend Louise Parsons. She said the "chickens" all stood off in a bunch and ran up to the witch

to tease her. "One of 'em is the witch and she stands
off—she's supposed to be washing her foot."

The chickens sing:

> Chicky, ma chicky, ma craney crow,
> Went to the well to wash her toe,
> What time, old witch?

> [Witch] One o'clock.

> Then you go and say it over again—

> Chicky, ma chicky, ma craney crow,
> Went to the well to wash her toe,
> What time, old witch?

> [Witch] Three o'clock.

And that time the witch tries to catch one, see? And that
one becomes the witch. She makes up the time—whoever's
the witch, and when they say *that* time she chases them. But
you got to guess the time. Like the first time I said "one
o'clock"—well, she don't pay no attention to that.

A favorite game with the boys was:

HUL GUL

(Tom McKinnon's version):

You've got both pockets full, bulged out, with chinquapins.
So you grab some in your hand and hide them, and you try
to fool them with how many you've got. Then you hold out
your hand:

> The other person says: "Hully Gully."

> Boy with chinquapins: "How many?"

Other person: "Four." (Guesses a number)

      Boy: "Four, you said, and six it is,
           Give me two to make it six."

(Or if the person had guessed six when the boy just had three in his hand, it would have gone like this):

Other person: "Six."

      Boy: "Six you said and three it was,
           Give me three to make it six."

(If the person guesses wrong he has to forfeit the difference. If he guesses right he gets all the chinquapins that the boy has in his hand.)

In the early days the school lunch program consisted of whatever was in the child's lunchpail, usually cold biscuits and leftovers. Aunt Chat remembered that she would take her lunch "in a big old bucket. We'd take cabbage and beans and biscuits and cornbread—whatever Ma had cooked up the day before." In recalling her school lunches Polly said she "took it in a bucket. Mama dried a lot of fruit and she would make us pies, half-moon pies, you know. And we had sorghum cookies. And sometimes she would bake us cakes and put this dried fruit between the layers of this cake. Oh, that was fun. We had the best food in the world."

To get to school Polly said they had to walk two and a half miles, with a mile of it across a lonely mountain. She shuddered as she recalled, "We had to leave home in the wintertime before daylight to get to school by eight o'clock. And the wolves at night would howl over on our school trail. And we had to go along there the next morning by daylight."

Restroom facilities in the schools were often primitive. Roy Simpson remembered the teacher standing up the first day and saying: " 'Now if the boys want to take a walk

The facilities were primitive.

you go over here to the woods to the south, and if the girls want to take a walk you go over here to the woods to the north.'" Soon, "the woods to the north were cleared off and they built the girls a house, but we Confederates to the south—we never did have one." At another school they built one big outhouse for both boys and girls—with a partition between the two sides. One day a little boy went out to the restroom and realized there was a girl on the other side, so he got a board and reached under the seat and gave her a swat on the bottom.

Another nonexistent feature was air conditioning or fans. Aunt Willie explained how they got around this. "The spring was near the school. They took a bucket of water from the spring for everyone to get a drink—they passed the bucket and each child took out a dipperful. In hot weather when someone didn't drink all of their dipperful they threw the remainder on the floor to help cool off the room."

There were no field trips as such, but school was dismissed for various *important* occasions:

—When Tinnie and Linnie thought they saw an old man with a long beard drop a tiny baby with a big rock tied around its neck into the pond at Hag's Holler, the school turned out to drag the pond.

—In Belleville many people still recall how Professor Montgomery dismissed school and everyone walked the mile into town to see the first train come through. The people on the train threw money out of the windows for the children to grab; and whole families came down from the mountains in wagonloads to see the train go by.

—During sorghum-making time the school on Chickalah Mountain dismissed classes and the children all went to the nearby sorghum mill where they got to dip paddles into the skimmings as a special treat.

—Aunt Willie recalled that, "One summer there wasn't any school on the mountain, but the neighbors got together and decided they'd have a tuition school at a little log church. One Friday afternoon a man came driving up in a hack and he had a load of watermelons that he had put in the cellar to cool. And he had enough for every child to have a half a melon. So we dismissed school and spent the afternoon eating watermelons."

A big school occasion was the last day of the term, with debates, recitations, a picnic, and a spelling match. The students also competed in "ciphering matches." Mrs. Joyce said they picked two leaders who chose sides and then one person from each team went to the blackboard to work the problems until one of them missed. Then the loser's side sent up another challenger. The challenger got to choose not only the type of problem (addition, subtraction, multiplication, or division) but could also say, "Multiply by two numbers; multiply by three numbers," etc. They kept on until one side ran out of people.

Many people in their eighties can still recite their favorite "speakin' piece" and can spell in the unusual syllable-by-syllable method that they used in their childhood. To do this the teacher would give out the spelling word and the speller would respond in a rapid, singsong manner, combining syllables as he went along. At eighty-seven Aunt Edna sounds like she's speaking a foreign language as she flies through words like: i-n in, c-o-m com incom, p-a-t pat imcompat, i eh imcompati, b-i-l bil incompatibil, i ah incompatibili, t-y tē incompatibility.

Farmer Wilhite remembered a technique called "singing the vowels" that they learned in their one-room schoolhouse. It was used to keep the children from slurring over the words without pronouncing the syllables—and he credits it with the clear enunciation that he has today. Taking each consonant, the children added it to a vowel and sang a little verse:

> B-a- bā
> B-e- bē
> B-i bī bic-a-bi
> B-o bō bic-a-bi-bo
> B-u bū bic-a-bi-bo-bu

In those days, as today, the schools were always in need of money, and a favorite fund-raising event was the box supper. This was usually the grand finale of the whole year and John Gideon recalled that:

> The teacher would announce the time and place and every woman and girl would fix a box supper for two people. These were auctioned off by the teacher. Usually each man bought his favorite girl's box. Sometimes they would bring as high as twenty-five dollars, and this was the talk of the country.

At times the results were almost tragic for a young man, as in this instance described by H. D. Payne:

> One time I went to the box supper at the school. And see, the highest bidder would get this box. Well, there was a girl there named Beulah Kane. She put one up on a shelf, and I just knew it was hers. So I started biddin' on it. I bid the last dollar I had, ten dollars I believe it was. I bid the last dollar I had—if it'd been a nickel more I couldn't a got it. Well, to cap it all—it was a married woman's with an old man there and seven kids. And I had to sit down and eat supper with them!

THE WATER MILL

Happy is the miller boy who lives by the mill,
The mill turns around with a free good will,
One hand in the hopper and the other in the sack,
The ladies step forward and the gents fall back.
                (Play-Party Game remembered by John Gideon)

One hundred years ago water mills were considered an absolute necessity in some parts of Arkansas. Today they have almost vanished from the scene. Occasionally, along a backwoods road in the mountains, a traveler may suddenly come upon the remains of an old waterwheel. As he stops to admire the picturesque setting he can imagine the laughter of earlier voices above the sounds of the water rushing over the rocks.

In the days when houses were isolated from each other, a trip to the mill to have the corn ground meant a chance for visiting with the neighbors and an opportunity to catch up on the gossip and swap tall tales. The millpond was sometimes used for baptizings, and the mill itself was often used as a voting place on election day. It was also a place where disputes were settled—one way or another. Fred

The wheel at Big Springs.

High told about the time his parents went to visit some neighbors, and after they were there awhile the wife suddenly shouted, "Oh, oh, here is John's knife. He left it

The Boxley Mill, its meal box, and its center beam of solid oak.

when he went to mill this morning and I'm afraid he will get into a fight and have nothing to defend himself with."

Mills began over 2,000 years ago and were carried by the Romans to Britain. The English brought the idea to the United States and the settlers brought them west to Arkansas. As the state became more and more populated mills were built along most of the streams. In 1840 the old Boxley Mill was built in the Upper Buffalo River Valley by a settler from South Carolina. Shortly afterward it was taken over by another settler, Samuel Whiteley of Virginia. By 1870 the original mill had been torn down and a larger mill built on the site. The second mill is still owned, but no longer operated, by Mr. Clyde Villines, the grandson of Samuel Whiteley's brother, Hezekiah.

The mill was built out of hewn logs that were put together with wooden pegs and covered with boards. The center beam of the first floor is one solid white oak log, forty feet long. Inside the three-story building everything is dusty and unused. There is a toll box lying beside the stone burrs used for grinding cornmeal. Mr. Villines said that in the old days they took a full toll box out of each bushel of corn and kept this "toll corn" in a nearby box. When the meal box was filled they ground that corn and

*Uncle Sam Hess at his hand mill. This recalls the story told by
Fred High:*
   "*Grandpap High had a hand mill that you could make meal out of
   corn and people would come with a poke of corn to grind. One day
   a young man and wife come and went to making meal. And he
   was in a hurry and was cranking the machine with all his might.
   and the wife was looking on. And she said, 'Don't, Jim, don't.
   You'll shake the pup out.' And the Highs did not know what she
   meant 'till they found out that they had come by another house and
   was given a pup—and he was carrying it in his shirt bosom.*"

sold the meal. Although the mill is silent now he
remembered that once there were "rush days" when they
had toe sacks of corn stacked all over the floor and they
ground a bushel every six minutes.

   Nearby there is a big pond filled by an underground
spring. At one time this spring was channeled into a sluice
and went through gates that controlled the water. One tall
fisherman's tale that has often been told says that when the
early pioneers arrived in Arkansas they found the streams
so full of fish that the fish clogged up the wheels of their
mills. That never quite happened at Boxley, but Mr.
Villines remembered how a five- or six-pound eel would
sometimes get in the sluice and get stuck in the
waterwheel, because the eel's hide was too tough to cut.

   The mills went by various genre names: "water mill"
referred to the type of power used: "grain mill," "grist
mill," and "flour mill" referred to the type of processing
that went on (usually these were combined in one
mill—certain days of the week were "corn days" and other
days were "wheat days"). "Burr mill" referred to the stone
(and later, metal) burrs that were used to grind the grain.

   In addition, many mills used their waterpower for
making thread, carding wool, and even distilling. In Van
Buren County at the Hunter Mill the "corn was ground or
liquefied as one might desire." Farmer Wilhite told how, in

his community, the waterpower from the same millpond was used by the grist mill, the cotton gin, and the sawmill. As he said, "Waterpower was all the power they had." If the water in back of the dam got too low, "they wouldn't saw a plank or gin a bale of cotton until the corn was ground because they knew the people had to eat. They'd always save at least some water to run the mill to grind the corn."

The mill at Boxley, the old grist mill in Mountain View, and the stave mill at Leslie are all deserted and not open to the public. One mill that has been restored and is open and easy to locate is the Old Spring Mill, built in 1867 just northwest of Batesville. And the grist mill that originally stood near Ozan and turned out "the best meal in Southwest Arkansas" has been moved to nearby Old Washington State Park, where it is part of a restored plantation.

Despite the fact that most of the mills have gone, they have left their mark in the names of towns all over the state. Dutch Mills, Eagle Mills; James Mill, Ferguson Mills, War Eagle Mills, and Jones Mill are just a few of the towns that remind us how important the mills once were to the people of Arkansas.

THE SALOON AND THE STILLS

In the early days almost every neighborhood had a little distillery and many towns had a saloon. The saloon was often located at the edge of town, due to the "three-mile law" that said no one could sell liquor within three miles of a church. Most of the whiskey in the saloons came from the local "wildcatter" and the wise man never located the source of his liquor. As Roy Simpson put it, "I very carefully never saw a still although I've been within a hundred yards of one."

This windowless saloon in Stone County was built more than one hundred years ago.

Today saloons are almost extinct in the mountains (since many of the counties are "dry") and moonshining has almost disappeared. But in case you are in the woods and accidentally come upon a still I will pass along the good advice some neighbors gave to Farmer Wilhite's parents when the Wilhites moved to Montgomery County in 1903.

Now they try to keep the stills concealed as much as possible, but sometimes, why, they think it's concealed and it isn't. The worst thing to do is to get scared and run, and especially if you've got a gun. Now you'll no doubt be scared, but don't act it—if you act scared and run you're liable to get shot. Cause even if you don't see anybody around there they see you.

You just go on up—if you got a gun you set it on the ground—lean it against a tree. Leave the gun and walk on

over to the still, and the thing for you to do is to first look at
the fire. Now they can't have too big a fire on that or it'll
overcook it. But stir the fire up a little and maybe put in
one small stick. And then you go to the mash barrel and
you stir that a little. And smell of it—you pull the paddle up
and smell of it. Then if there's anything dripping out of the
worm into the jar—there'll be a tin cup there—you stick the
tin cup under the drip, and you catch a little drip and you
smell of it. Then you take a sip or make out like you're
takin' a sip of it. It might knock you down if you took a sip,
but just make out like you're tastin' it.

Then just act casual and you walk on over and get your
gun and you walk on off. Now see, in the first place you
can't prosecute them and you can't be witness against
them—because you helped with the thing. You helped
build the fire, you stirred the mash, and you checked the
drip. You've done enough so you've helped make the stuff
and so they're safe from you.

THE GENERAL STORE

The general store in each little town was one of the
gathering places for the surrounding area. It was the spot
where the men collected on Saturday afternoons to swat
flies and swap lies, to spit and to whittle. As they hunkered
outside, trading stories, their wives went inside to get the
mail and trade their farm produce for a few store-bought
goods. An advertisement in the *Arkansas Gazette* of 1819
gives an idea of the merchandise they could expect to find.
Lewis and Thomas offered for sale in their store "a
complete and general assortment of dry-goods, groceries,
hardware, Queens-ware, books, stationery, saddles and
trunks." They were prepared to furnish "Lee's Celebrated
Patent and Family Medicines," and daily expected a
shipment from Philadelphia which would include "Ladies
Beaver hats, with and without feathers." On a smaller
scale, Aunt Willie recalled that in Belleville one of the

going items was a brain-workers' tonic, "suitable for teachers."

Even into this century bartering was commonplace. The women brought in their butter, eggs, chickens, and berries; and the men brought the roots they had dug and the hides and meat from the game they had killed.

When people lived in areas too remote to get to the store, the store went to them in the form of a peddler. From the earliest days, when there were only trails to the homes, the "pack peddler" or "foot peddler" came with all his goods in a pack on his back. As roads were cleared, a new kind of salesman, called the "chicken peddler," made the rounds. He is described by Farmer Wilhite, who remembers them from his early days in the Ouachita Mountains.

> We was really way out there in the woods and stores was few and far between. The women never got to go to any store or anything, so they had what they'd call "chicken peddlers." A feller would fix up a wagon with a lot of compartments and so on, where he could carry some bolts of cloth and pots and pans, thread, and oh, it's a wonder the amount of different things that they could carry. Well, they depended for their pay on chickens and eggs and farm produce of that kind. So the women'd save up their eggs and have some chickens in a coop and different things that they'd swap to this chicken peddler for his goods. He made a livin' out of it and they could swap gossip from all around.

The Grant County peddler was a black man named Uncle Adam Garvin. According to Sim Goodman: "In the early days Uncle Adam ran a peddlin' wagon. He drove the wagon and carried a little soap and needles and thread and a little calico and gingham and stuff around. And peddled it. In exchange he'd take chickens and eggs and hides and anything you had—dried fruit or anything—in exchange for these things he sold. And he made the

Saturday afternoon at Leslie. The sidewalk is covered with shavings the whittlers have left.

rounds over the county. That was his peddlin' wagon. He carried sardines and raisins and stuff like that. And the white people respected him and bought from him." And Uncle Adam must have enjoyed his work since he lived to be one hundred and seven years old!

To draw the crowds to town the small-town merchants came up with a number of "attractions," many of which are still used. One was a "drawing" on Saturday afternoon. The names of everyone in the town and surrounding area were put in a box and each week a name was drawn to receive the week's prize.

Two old customs that draw the crowds to town are still held in many places. One is "swappin' days," where everyone brings their white elephants to trade for someone else's. The other is the local auction, with the quick-thinking auctioneer promising such nonsense things as: "This table has solid wooden legs," or (when he has a single old spur rather than a pair), "This spur belonged to a one-legged bandit." Recently, while auctioning the contents of a country store, an auctioneer took advantage of the rivalry between the two football teams, the University of Arkansas Razorbacks and the University of Texas Longhorns. When he came to a box of thirty plates decorated with pictures of the Razorback Hog and saying, "Arkansas—Land of Opportunity," he called out, "Step right up, ladies and gentlemen. Buy this box of beautiful plates and have all your Christmas shopping done. Send one to all your friends in Texas!"

Despite all the attractions that were offered, the health of the store depended on the health of the town. One woman remembered the closing days of Rush, a mining community that is now a ghost town. Her dad owned the general store and she recalled that at the last, "It was not a going place. The men sat on the porch and eat out of a can and just talked."

Finally, when cars and better roads became common, the country store gave way to the shopping center. One

old storekeeper in northern Arkansas summed up the
problems when he told how people would drive past his
store and go eight miles into Missouri to do their
shopping—just to have someplace to go in their brand-
new cars. As mail delivery increased, the people didn't
even have to go to the store to get their mail. Roy Simpson
remarked sadly, "The thing that really tore the fabric of it
was the car . . . . They've built the Emerson Motors
where the Salyer Livery Barn stood." And Fred High
admitted: "My trade grew worse and worse as roads got
better . . . . So, good roads, cars, and rural routes put
me out of business."

Unfortunately, when the general store died out one
excellent old custom went with it. As Farmer Wilhite told
about the following practice I couldn't help thinking how
nice for our ecology it would have been if this custom had
remained:

> Everything wasn't put up in cans and bottles like it is
> today. They had barrels and bins and used them over and
> over. And you brought your own container; they didn't
> have no grocery bags or things. You brought your own
> bucket—or jug if you were gonna get some molasses or
> vinegar—and they put it in *your* container.

CHURCHES

When they go to meetin', I'll tell you what they wear,
Their old duckin' pants, all pitched and tear,
Their old cotton socks that they'd wore the winter
    round
And their old coarse boots with the tops turned down,
And their old leather hat more brim than crown.
                        (From "The Arkansas Boys")

"Goin' to meetin'" was a favorite activity, and as the
pioneers moved into the state the churches multiplied.

This church in the Ozarks has everything a country church should have: a big shade tree on the lawn with tables set up underneath, a steeple with a bell, and a graveyard with lambs on the stones.

Patience recalled that, "We had singing on Tuesday night and prayer meetin' on Wednesday night and church all day long on Sunday. They even carried the chilluns to church, you see, and they learnt 'em church."

For a look at Arkansas folk customs there is no better place to turn than to the activities of these small community churches. At a time when roads to the courthouse were poor and social occasions were scarce, the congregation of the church often served as judge and juror; while the meeting house was a social center as well as a place for repenting, baptizing, marrying, and burying.

Many of the folk sayings that we use today came from the church. A person who agrees with another often says, "I'm sittin' in the Amen corner." When someone has everything organized he will say, "Now I've got everybody in the same pew," and when he sees a friend all dressed up he'll say, "Where ya preachin', John?" or "I didn't recognize you in your Sunday-go-to-meetin' clothes." An executive may send for an employee to "call him up on the carpet," but Aunt Alma says that in the old days it was the sinner about to be turned out of the church who was called up on the piece of carpet at the front of the sanctuary.

CHURCH RECORD BOOKS

To see how truly all-inclusive the early church was in the lives of the people, nothing can beat a look at the old Minute Books. The people were "turned out," "excused from the church," or "excluded from fellowship" for legal, moral, and social reasons, as well as religious causes. Most of these were listed in the record books as "unchristian conduct," with a "specification" such as "swearing," "dancing," "selling hogs that did not belong to him," "drunkedness," "engaging in social parties," and "belonging to a secret organization."

In addition, disciplinary action was taken for nonpayment of debts, roving eyes, swinging hips, and a variety of family causes, as seen in these old church records:

—February, 1873. "The case of Sister Bradshaw was taken up that was referred to a committee on last meeting, and committee reported satisfied. Then there was an objection raised again for not satisfying W. J. Wiggins for a debt and was excused. On objection the church gave her until April meeting to satisfy W. J. Wiggins." (In April the "case of Sister Bradshaw taken up and she failing to satisfy' Brother Wiggins was excused from church.")

—July, 1873. "Taking up reports against Sister Chandler, who had during services turned in her seat and with a roving eye, looked back over the congregation. Heard by motion and seconded, church agreed to send three Sisters to examine the case."

—November, 1873. "Called on two of the Brothers of the congregation to visit with a Brother, his wife, and another Sister and report at the next meeting. Charges were that the two women, Sister Suggs and Sister Harkey, swung their hips in an unusual manner when walking." In February of the following year Sister Harkey was "acquitted" (notice the legal language) and six months later Sister Suggs was "acquitted after her acknowledgement to 'evil walk.'" (The way that people walked apparently presented a real problem to the churches. In June, 1889, the Big Creek Deacons "reported to the church that some of the Brethren had been walking disordily of late," and in September, 1897, the Chickalah Mountain Church minutes state, "Charge taken up against Sister Tucker for disorderly walk and she was excluded from fellowship of church.")

Family problems were also handled by committees of the church, as in May, 1875. "Told by Brother Lowrey that he and Sister Lowrey had separated as man and wife; took up case by appointing committee of three Brothers to visit them and report at next meeting." In August of the same year the church at Magazine Mountain sent a letter to the church on Chickalah Mountain pointing out the disorderly conduct of another one of the Brothers who was separated from his wife, and the church "on motion agreed to his disorders and ordered him to lay down his guilt." However, in September he and his wife had reconciled and "he was acquitted."

When the deacons of the church were not "hearing the evidence" and excluding the sinners from fellowship, they were busy appointing each other to numerous committees. Every time a member sinned, a visiting committee of three or four persons was established to apprise the erring Brother or Sister of the fact that he or she had been excluded and urge repentance.

Also, there were multitudes of standing committees. Just a few of those mentioned by one church were: the Committee on Church House building; various "subscription" committees (including one appointed to "Rase funds to Pay our Pastor"); a Committee to Purchase (eight) New Hymn Books; a committee to have new seats made for the church—referred to afterward as the Seat Committee; a Grave Yard Committee; a "Committee to have the well dug"; and a "Committee for Solisiting New Members."

CHURCH SOCIALS

In addition to the regular church meetings, there were numerous social gatherings at the church. One of the traditions that began with the most primitive brush arbor and is still thriving today is the church supper. In the old days this was often a fund-raising event, since the church budgets were usually meager. (The Mt. Magazine Church reported a budget with $1.30 in the treasury in 1851.) The food for the supper was donated by the ladies of the church, who outdid themselves showing off their culinary skills. A small sum was charged for the dinner and the proceeds went to the building fund or to supplement the salary of the badly underpaid minister. (In December, 1885, the Subscription Committee of the Big Creek Church at Sheridan raised a total of $18 to pay the preacher for the previous year.)

Another church activity that most older people remember was the custom of "poundings" or "donation parties." This was a type of housewarming held when a new minister and his family came to the community. The congregation held a get-together for them and each person brought a pound of some staple to fill the preacher's larder.

Mrs. Hardgrave recalled: "They would just take different things, you know. Like a pound of coffee or a pound of meal—just a lot of food like that. And they called it a pounding. It didn't make any difference what you took. Just anything you wanted to take 'cause people can use everything, you know."

The wealthier members brought more than their one pound of flour and the small children often brought only a bouquet of wild flowers, but it was an excellent excuse for a party and a chance to get to know the new minister and his wife better. Like the church supper, the pounding also served the purpose of supplementing the preacher's salary.

Today this custom has almost died out, but still survives in a few country churches. Frances Petrovicz described the poundings they have at their small church in Alpena:

We have the pounding each time a new preacher arrives to preach at our church. We might even have the pounding for each new year he stays.

We have our monthly fellowship supper second Monday of each month at which time the preacher and his family also attend. When he starts his year of preaching we set the date of the pounding first supper after that.

The congregation brings anything they wish in foodstuffs—garden produce, fresh fruit, eggs, staple goods such as coffee, sugar, meal, or frozen meats and canned goods. We gather this in one lot in boxes and bags. We delegate someone to make a short speech of presentation, generally a man, after we have our supper. In turn, the preacher and his wife express their thanks. We then either visit, sing hymns, or have short meetings or commissions.

One of the favorite dishes for any church social was a Bible cake or Scripture cake. Below is one of the many recipes for this. For the Bible-reading women of yester-year the only part necessary was the amount and name of each scripture, but for the modern reader I have included the ingredients and the text of each scripture.

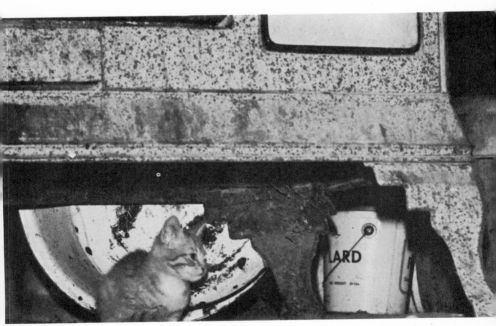

Under the wood-burning stove—waiting for a piece of Bible cake?

BIBLE CAKE

1 c. Judges 5:25—butter—"she brought forth butter in a lordly dish."

2 c. Jeremiah 6:20—sugar—"To what purpose cometh there to me incense from Sheba, and the sweet cane from a far country?"

2 t. I Samuel 14:25—honey—"And all they of the land came to a wood; and there was honey upon the ground."

6 Jeremiah 17:11—eggs—"As the partridge sitteth on eggs, and hatcheth them not";

4½ c. I Kings 4:22—flour—"And Solomon's provision for one day was thirty measures of fine flour,"

2 heaping t. Amos 4:5—baking powder—"And offer a sacrifice of thanksgiving with leaven."

1 c. I Samuel 30:12—raisins—"And they gave him a piece of a cake of figs, and two clusters of raisins";

1 c. Nahum 3:12—figs—"All thy strong holds shall be like fig trees with the first-ripe figs."

to taste—II Chronicles 9:9—spices—"And she gave the king an hundred and twenty talents of gold, and of spices great abundance."

Cream butter, sugar, and honey. Beat eggs until frothy. (Sometimes this part is simply stated as, "Follow Solomon's prescription for making a good boy—Proverbs 23:14—'Thou shalt beat him with the rod.') Add milk, then cream the mixture. Sift dry ingredients. Chop raisins and figs and flour them before adding. Bake at 350 degrees until set. This makes a very large and heavy cake.

FIFTH SUNDAY AND FASOLA

Dear Sister Morgan: Please announce in the Trumpet that there will be a fifth Sunday meeting in December at First Primitive Baptist church on Gardner Lane, Hot Springs, Ark. Services will begin Saturday morning at 10:00 o'clock and continue through Saturday afternoon, evening and Sunday. We wish to invite all who can to come and be with us. And those of you who cannot come, please pray the Lord of heaven will be with us.

Opal J. O'Neal, church clerk
(*Baptist Newsletter,* 1972)

Any time there was a fifth Sunday in the month it was a special time in all the country churches. Often several congregations got together for a two-day meeting or at least an all-day singing with dinner on the grounds. In April, 1893, the minutes of the Big Creek Church (Grant County) recorded that "Four of the Brothers were appointed messengers to the Fifth Sunday Meeting of the Pine Bluff Association." This custom still persists in many churches today.

On September 30, 1973, Patience was busy getting ready for her Fifth Sunday meeting. She attends the Zion Chapel at Scott, but she said that on the fifth Sunday, "We go to the Mission Church and call it Mission Sunday and everybody wears white. We has dinner—four churches get together—and then we all sing and say prayers and poems and things." When I asked her why she wasn't dressed in white, she said, "I'm gonna carry my white dress over to the church." (She explained that they have a service at their own church first and then go over to the Mission Church. Only the women wear white.)

In April, 1972, Mrs. Petrovicz of Alpena (the Ozarks) wrote: "Tonight is our Fifth Sunday, at which time the preacher will not have a sermon and anybody contributes their talents in singing, reciting, or group singing."

Patience and friends at a Fifth Sunday service.

Less common today than in earlier years is the use of the shape-note songbooks at the·Fifth Sunday singing. During the 1800's and early 1900's, singing schools were held in most of the rural communities to teach the people of all ages this system of four (and later, seven) syllable solmization. They have been referred to as Fasola Folks, Buckwheat Note Singers, and Sacred Harpers (after one of their favorite song books); but no matter what their titles, they have a long and interesting history that has been traced back to Elizabethan times in England.

Around 1770 the "singing-school" movement began in New England and was carried into the frontier of the South by way of the Yankee singing-school masters who traveled from town to town. In each town the singing-school teacher secured a place to hold his lessons; and with nothing more than a blackboard, chalk, and his songbook with the rudiments in the front, he taught the people to sing.

First, all the songs were sung using only the names of the notes (fa-sol-la, fa-sol-la, mi), and then the words were introduced. Even today when it is time to "raise the hymn" the leader will begin beating time with his right hand and the singers will "note" the hymn all the way through before they sing the words.

Shape-note singing was an emotional as well as a musical experience. Stamps-Baxter's *Modern Rudiments of Music* states that each tone is to be of a different "Kind or Character" and divides them into "Clear Tones" (expressing "Tranquility, cheerfulness, gaity, boldness, exhaltation, joy, and courage") and "Somber Tones" (expressing "Sadness, grief, awe, fear, solemnity, and devotion").

Because many of the people could not read or did not own hymn books, the leader would often "line out" the hymns. He would call out two lines at a time and the congregation would sing them back to him. Added to this was an unusual custom that Gerstaeker noted several times in his travels through Arkansas: "The preacher stood up to sing, and the congregation joined in the singing, turning their backs to him."

After years of four-note singing, the more modern school of seven-note singing arose. Some writers who made their living producing tune books clung stubbornly to the old style, but others were more realistic. In the book *White Spirituals in the Southern Uplands,* George Pullen Jackson told how "Singin' Billy" Walker declared that he had knelt in prayer and received a revelation from God that caused him to switch from four-shapes to seven-shapes. "Singin' Billy" further justified his switch by saying that there were seven distinct sounds on the scale, and he wondered, "Would any parent having seven children, ever think of calling them by only four names?"

Today the Sacred Harp singing has become a living tradition in some parts of Arkansas. The people who carry on these homespun songs or "folk hymns" are keeping vital not only a way of music, but an entire way of life. One of these is Roland Gillihan, who has been teaching shape-note singing in Stone County for twenty-two years. His singing schools last ten nights at a time, Monday through Friday, for two weeks. All ages come to his lessons, which are usually held in the churches or the schools. In his area of the Ozarks the singing-school is still important, since, as he claims, "Most everyone except the piano players around here, they go by these shape notes. Flatwoods, out here, they have the round notes; but most all the other churches around here use the shape-note books."

For his school all he needs is a blackboard, chalk, and a copy of the rudiments for each student. Then he explains his procedure:

I have a four-by-eight blackboard. I put this scale right here on my blackboard and I drill them in that scale upward and down.

do   re   mi   fa   ' sol   la   te

It's always do when you see that shape. When I'm teaching I call that [re] the washkettle. Mi is the diamond; fa the triangle; then the oval, that's sol; la, the rectangle; te is the ice cream cone; and do the pyramid. Do is always your home tone—except in the minors la is your home tone.

The main idea is learning that every time this sol appears anywhere in this music it has the same pitch. Whenever you learn to read those notes, why you can just sing the melody and then turn right around and sing the words to that same melody and you've got it right.

Those seven notes, with all their different lengths and intermediate tones—all the music in the world is built around them.

FUNERALS

Although not intended as social occasions, baptisms, protracted meetings, and even funerals, were opportunities for people to get together at the church and visit with friends and relatives who lived far away. A large baptism at the river or a well-known preacher at a revival could lead to the social high point of the year in a small community, with supper on the lawn and a huge crowd of people who might not otherwise darken the door of the church from year to year.

Even funerals were social events. My neighbor told how she used to visit at a country house next to a negro cemetery where the funerals lasted all day with dinner served at noon. The funerals were held so long after the actual burial that they were more like big homecomings, and the part she remembered best was the little boy who

would always be there selling cold drinks and calling out
all during the funeral, "Sody pop, sody pop, ice cold sody
pop."

Patience remembered how they . . .

> Buried 'em next day. Had to bury 'em that next day
> because you see they didn't mortify 'em.
>
> Have funeral—way, oh, sometime like I die now they'd
> have my funeral 'bout next year sometime. I often thinks
> about that —I don't know what they waited for. I know
> they'd buy fine dresses and everything for the funeral—
> they'd say 'fixin' for the funeral.' The funerals lasted all
> day—had dinner at the church. They'd be 'celebratin' for
> the dead.' They'd have the funeral at the church—way
> afterwards.

This was a common practice in many parts of the South,
and the *Southern Folklore Quarterly* related that in Kentucky
during the pioneer days the funeral was held when the
preacher could come, which sometimes meant that years
passed between the burying and the funeral. According to
a Kentucky funeral notice, a funeral was held for a man
and four of his deceased wives, all at the same time.

The preparation for the burial was a community effort,
from the "laying out" of the body to the making of the
coffin. It was interesting to see how similar the burial
customs in the white communities of the mountains were
to the customs of the black communities of the plantations.
Aunt Chat remembered:

> They'd be somebody in the settlement that could make
> coffins and that's what they did. They had to make 'em
> all—they was no bought coffins. They'd take pine lumber
> and they'd make 'em—I guess you've seen the pictures—
> where they'd shape in this way [at the top] and then bend
> and shape in to the foot. They was wider at the elbows.
>
> And they'd line 'em with white and cover 'em with black.
> And sometimes they'd get black lace and put on to come

over the black, and white lace to go on over the white—just
narrow little lace to tack over the edge of the inch pine
lumber.

Mrs. Hoggard told of similar customs in Faulkner
County:

> Just any of the neighbor men could make the coffins.
> They made 'em out of lumber—light lumber, you
> know—and covered them with black cloth and then lined
> them with white. And they made the little pillows and all to
> go in them. And if they wanted 'em kind of fixed up they'd
> buy silver outfits to put on 'em.
>
> They sat up with 'em when they got sick—you know,
> they'd go to the homes. Different neighbors'd go there—
> some would go one night and some the next night. And
> then when they died they laid 'em out—right in one room.
> And a crowd would go there and set up with the dead. And
> they'd take 'em to the graveyard in a wagon.

Patience recalled:

> People made the coffins outta planks. They was
> sharp—so sharp. They made 'em to fit your feet—you
> know, they'd be little down here and big in the middle
> and little up at your head. And we children called 'em
> *toothpicks*—we didn't know no better.
>
> We didn't have no undertakers then. We had to sit up
> with the dead folks. We'd stay with 'em all night—you
> know, sit with the family. We called that wakes.

Aunt Chat told about an eerie experience she had one
night when she was sitting up with the body of a girl who
had died in her neighborhood. The men in the family had
gone off to make the coffin and Aunt Chat and a friend
were the only ones left to sit with the body.

> When it begin to get about three or four o'clock it
> seemed like die I would. Those cats! It was an old log house

and the plank was out here. She was laid out over there and the plank was outta the ceilin' too. And them cats'd climb them walls and get up there and they'd look down with the awfullest eyes, and just squall. They'd want on that corpse. Now we'd have to keep them minded off-a that corpse. And about three o'clock they got the coffin finished—over at Uncle Leonard Liles's. And they brought it to put the body in. Oh, I was so glad when they come with that coffin, I didn't know what to do. And they can make the awfullest, squallinest racket you ever heard when they're after a corpse that way.

Today the body is rushed to a funeral home where a coffin is purchased and the funeral is held in two or three days. Other funeral customs are changing, too. Since the earliest days people meeting a funeral procession on the road have always stopped until the procession passed. In July, 1973, the Arkansas Funeral Directors Association joined with the State Police in asking motorists to please discontinue this custom. They noted that it was "a long-standing practice thought to show respect for the deceased" but that it had "originated before high-speed highways." They went on to state that there had been a number of accidents when "approaching motorists stopped and others following them didn't." To smooth the transition for custom-bound folks they suggested that, "If the approaching motorist would slow their speed upon the approach of a funeral procession this would indicate the desired respect for the deceased and would be much safer for the drivers in the funeral procession as well as the other motorists on the highway."

When Mrs. Wilhite was a little girl her mother often sang a song called "Who Killed Cock Robin?" to her. As Mrs. Wilhite sang it for me it made me realize how many of the funeral customs, from the making of the shroud to the tolling of the bell, have disappeared. Here is the song as she sang it:

Who killed Cock Robin?
Who killed Cock Robin?
I, said the sparrow,
With my bow and arrow.
Twas I, twas I, twas I, O.

Who saw him die?
Who saw him die?
I, said the fly,
With my little eye.
Twas I, twas I, twas I, O.

Who caught his blood?
Who caught his blood?
I, said the fish,
With my little dish.
Twas I, twas I, twas I, O.

Who dug his grave?
Who dug his grave?
I, said the crow,
With my grubbing hoe.
Twas I, twas I, twas I, O.

Who covered him up?
Who covered him up?
I, said the duck,
With my silver cup.
Twas I, twas I, twas I, O.

Who told the news?
Who told the news?
I, said the bull,
Just as hard as I could pull.
I—rang—the news.

Who made his shroud?
Who made his shroud?
I, said the beetle,
With my thread and needle.
Twas I, twas I, twas I, O.

Who preached his funeral?
Who preached his funeral?
I, said the swallow,
Just as loud as I could holler.
Twas I, twas I, twas I, O.

CAMP MEETINGS

I went down a camp meeting the other afternoon
fer to hear them shout and sing,
And to tell each other how they loved one another
and to let hallelujahs ring.
. . . .
They catch up on the hands,
Start marching round a ring,
Keep a shouting all the while.
You'd think it was a cyclone a comin' through the air
You could hear them shout half a mile.

("Methodist Pie")

The grand culmination of the church year came at the end of the summer when everyone gathered for the camp meeting. This meeting was attended by all the people of one denomination in a large area, and was "arranged to commence the latter part of July or early weeks of August after the crops were laid by." It got its name from the fact that the people literally camped at the meeting site, since this "season of prayer" (as Cephas Washburn called it) lasted for days and even weeks.

This custom was described by one man as "the religious feature of the year, particularly among the Methodists" and today the Methodists are still going strong. A *Gazette* article in August, 1972, announced that "The Salem Camp

Meeting will hold its 118th annual session Friday through August 27 at the campground six miles northeast of Benton." The activities listed for those ten days included not only daily preaching and singing services, but a homecoming service and a memorial service.

In the early days the whole family and the milk cow went to camp meeting, leaving the farm to tend to itself. As one man wrote in a letter of 1876, ". . . we soon got thick enough to hold camp meeting and everybody would go and leave their houses for a week at a time. And when they came back everything was all right."

When they approached the campsite each family's wagon was loaded down with pots and pans, clothes and feather beds. As Aunt Chat recalled, "We'd water up the old wagonwheels and start plumb to Black Rock over that mountain. The wheels wouldn't stay on unless we water'd 'em and made 'em swell up—to keep 'em from runnin' off. Now we'd start to that camp meetin' and get to that mountain—not a very big team of horses—and we'd all walk over that mountain [ten miles]."

When they got there she went on to describe the site:

> They had little camp houses built here and there—and they'd cook out on benches. They made benches, you know, and had dirt throwed over 'em. They'd have 'em up high and then they'd build a fire on that and they'd cook on them. We'd stay a week at a time and then we'd go home and tend to things at home and then we'd go right back. And I mean of all the singing and the shouting and the good times—they had it! Pa could sing all night, and never look at a book, and never sing the same song twice.

Roy Simpson recalled that:

> You could tell who was gonna shout because it was the same people did it all the time. For instance, Savannah Agar at Highland—the girls used to follow and pick up her hairpins, and I've known her even to fall over to the floor

with her hair flying and she was shouting—and sometimes the men did too. But there were others that you couldn't have got to shout. It was an individual thing with them. A lot of folks never indulged in the shouting. If you felt like it—break out; if you didn't feel like it you didn't have to.

He went on to relate some problems that arose when not everyone approved of these meetings. When the Pentecostal movement came to the Ouachitas,

One man was holding a meeting over there in a community beyond Slick Rock Gap and he'd go over riding a mule. He started up Slick Rock Gap there one day and a Winchester went to cracking up there above him—the bullets whizzing around him. The fellow wasn't actually trying to hit him because *he could of hit him.* Roysten [the preacher] turned that mule around and someone said they saw him really urging that mule back up the road. This fellow's wife had gotten interested [in religion] and he didn't want her doing it. He just simply scared the preacher off.

In recalling camp meetings in town, Annie Campbell said, "We had them under tents. There would just be groups of people, and the skeeters'd nearly eat you up. They had smudge pots burning all around the tent till you couldn't hardly breathe. But I enjoyed it."

However, at most rural campsites the men got together and built a brush arbor before the meeting began. Today brush arbors can occasionally still be seen on remote country roads around the state. They are almost all identical. The old one they had fifty years ago in the Ouachita Mountains was described by Brother Lonzo Tallent and sounded like a description of the one that we saw in the Ozarks in 1972. Both of these were exactly like the one Patience remembered when she was a little girl down in the plantation country. This is the way she described it: "They put up postes in the woods and then

A brush arbor in Newton County.

cut little trees and throwed them up over the top of it, and
called it a brush harbor. And they'd have church under
there. Sat on them logs and stumps and things. Or they'd
make benches—have some planks and set on 'em.''

The high point of a camp meeting, or any revival
service, was the conversion of the sinful. This led to rivalry
among the denominations, and to the choice of sermon
topics such as "Believers Baptism—the *only* baptism taught
in the Bible" (title of a sermon to be delivered at a
protracted meeting at Big Creek Baptist Church.) The
following story, told in the *Biography of the Rev. Cephas
Washburn,* illustrates how early this rivalry began; for
Cephas Washburn began his missionary work to the
Indians in 1819.

Though the Indians are proverbial for their taciturnity
and gravity, they are said to be, at times, remarkable for
the keenness of their sarcasm. The people of the frontier
settlements, in early times, who owned cattle, were

accustomed to prepare what were usually called lick-logs.
These were simply fallen trees with notches cut in them a
few inches deep, and at the distance of two or three feet
apart. To these logs it was usual to repair once or twice a
week and salt the cattle. In this manner each man attended
his own flock, and was enabled to keep them separate from
others. The term "lick-log" was sometimes applied to
preaching places.

A Baptist minister and Mr. Washburn (who was a
Methodist) happened once to lodge together where a
number of Indians were present, and the conversation
turned upon the success of their respective labours. The
Baptist remarked that he had lately been favoured with
quite a revival at one of his preaching places among the
white people, and that a considerable number had united
with his church and been immersed. During the conversation he also stated that they had nearly all been members of
the Methodist Church.

"Oh," said Mr. Washburn, "then you and I attach
different ideas to the word revival. If those persons were
worthy members of the Methodist Church, I should
consider their connecting themselves with your church as
only a change of Church membership. By a revival I mean
a change of the heart from sin to holiness." "Well, however
that may be," replied the Baptist, "they come to my lick-log,
and I put my mark upon them."

An Indian present, who had been listening with deep
interest, as soon as he heard this remark, using the peculiar
shrug and ejaculation exclaimed, "If any man put his mark
upon my cattle when they go to his lick-log, I call him
cow-thief."

CHAPTER 5
FROLICS

As she sat in the kitchen churning, the farm wife sang:

> Come, butter, come.
> Come, butter, quick.
> For old Aunt Kate's
> A-waitin' at the gate
> For a piece of johnnycake,
> Come, butter, come.

While her husband, planting corn in the fields, was chanting:

> One for the worms
> One for the crow,
> One for to rot
> And one for to grow.*

*The churning song, sung by Granny Riddle, has been found in a similar form in Georgia (*A Treasury of Georgia Folklore*). The planting song, along with the custom of planting four times too many seeds in each spot, is found in England (*Discovering the Folklore of Plants*). There, the rhyme goes: "One to rot and one to grow, One for pigeon, one for the crow." Mrs. Essie Ward remembered a different planting chant that called for three seeds in each spot and said simply, "One to push, one to grunt, one to grow."

Whatever they were doing, the early settlers of Arkansas had a song to accompany themselves. Partly because of these songs, work and play were often intermingled for the pioneers. Corn huskings, log-rollings, house-raisings, and quilting bees all became a "frolic" in addition to getting the job done.

Farmer Wilhite recalled that, "In the country—when I was a boy—in the early fall, why, two or three neighbor families would get together and they'd help each other pick cotton and they sang and told tall tales while they picked cotton."

On his journey through Arkansas in the early 1800's Gerstaeker reported:

> In spring of the year, the so-called "frolics" are of common occurrence. Let us say a farmer wishes to clear a tract of land. After he has felled the trees and cut them into log lengths, he invites his neighbors to come and help roll the logs into heaps so that they may be burned. This is called a "log rolling frolic." If the farmer is married his wife arranges a "frolic" too. To this she invites her friends and the young girls from the neighborhood. Out of colored squares of calico they put a quilt together. This is called a "quilting frolic." In the evening after the work is done follows a dance or a play party.

Some of the events discussed in this section were purely for fun, others were primarily chores. But all were great diversions, as they gave the isolated people of the mountains a rare chance for a get-together.

SORGHUM-MAKING

> Sorghum-making was usually a joyful time of the year with the folks. We always looked forward to sorghum-making because usually you had done run out of sorghum by this time and you was glad to have some new syrup.
>
> (Farmer Wilhite)

In the old days almost every farmer had a sorghum patch to provide his family with some sweetening other than honey. Along about September the cane from the sorghum was made into molasses as a treat for the family, and the extra stalks were stored as a wintertime treat for the hogs.

Sorghum-making was a simple process. First, the outer leaves were stripped off the stalks with homemade paddles. Then the cane was cut and taken to the nearby sorghum mill where it was crushed in a cane press operated by mules, horses, or (today) tractors. The juice from the cane was cooked for hours until it was the right consistency for sorghum molasses.

Even though the weather was often too hot and the flies and bees came by the thousands, the early Arkansans always managed to make a festive occasion out of sorghum-making. They even laughed about the discomforts. One man told me the flies and the bees in his sorghum came free of charge, and another claimed the bees gave the sorghum its flavor. An old song said the sorghum got so full of flies "it looked like raisin pie," but no one seemed to mind.

Around the sorghum mill there was a special vocabulary. Some of the terms that are still used today include:

Paddle —This is a flat stick used to strip the sorghum stalks in the field. The farmer walks up and down the rows with a paddle in each hand, waving his arms like a windmill, stripping the leaves off the cane. Mr. Pledger said he preferred oak for his paddles because it would really "fight those leaves down" and wouldn't break if it accidentally hit the ground.

Rack—At the mill posts are driven into the ground several feet apart. The space between each set of posts is allotted to a certain man and he piles his cane there while waiting for it to be processed. This area is called a rack.

Pole and Press—This is another name for the mill itself.

Sorghum stacked at the mill.

Lee rides the sweep.

Mr. Pledger rests on a stack of pumice. A favorite game with the children was climbing to the top of the pumice pile and rolling to the bottom.

The pole (or sweep) is attached to the press and is turned by the mules on the other end. The press is made up of rollers that squeeze the juice out of the cane. Whenever possible the pole and press were put on a knoll so that the juice could run downhill through a hose or pipe, and didn't have to be carried to the furnace by hand.

Pumice—This is the roughage of the sorghum stalk that comes out the back of the press after the juice has been extracted.

Mr. Sumler's mules, Blue and Jude, have made a lot of sorghum in their day. Blue was thirty-five when this picture was made.

Juice—The juice is the green liquid that comes out of the cane and runs into a barrel next to the press. More than one man said, "I never make sorghum without drinkin' some of the juice."

Furnace—A wood-burning furnace, usually built of bricks, is set up near the mill. On top of the furnace is a long, partitioned pan where the juice is cooked into syrup. The pan is ten to twelve feet long and made of solid copper.

Rake—This is a wooden block on a long handle. It is used to push the juice along from section to section of the cooking pan.

Scum—The scum is the greenish foam that forms on top of the cooking sorghum.

Strainer—This is a pierced tin shovel that is used to skim the scum off the top of the sorghum as it cooks. Someone has to stand over the hot pan raking and straining the juice during the entire time that it is cooking.

Washing—Polly recalled that her daddy "had a way of 'washing' the cooking juice. When it got so far, he would take a cup of cold water and he'd just throw this cup of water the whole length of the pan and that cooled it. It'd quit boiling for a second or two. And that would throw those green skimmings to the end each time."

Testing—Farmer Wilhite described how they would test the syrup: "When the syrup looks thick enough, they pour up a glassful and then they set it in a pan of cold water.

Straining the juice through the burlap into the barrel.

Getting rid of the skimmings.

They let it set there for awhile. Then they take a spoon and stick it down in that glass, and if they can lift the glass and everything up by that spoon handle then that's sorghum. And that is good syrup, now, I'll tell you."

Long Sweetenin'—This is another name for sorghum molasses—to distinguish it from honey, which was "short sweetenin'." Sometimes the syrup was distilled into a drink called "monkey rum." As H. D. Payne said, molasses was even better if you "Let it set for awhile till it gets fermated."

Green Sorghum—If the sorghum is hurried off the fire too soon it remains green and runny. This is called green sorghum and is supposed to be bad for you. As one man

Cooking the syrup is a tiresome job.

said about sorghum that hadn't cooked long enough, "It warn't nothin' but hot juice."

Suckers—These are pieces of cane that people around the mill chew on or stick into the syrup to use as tasters. Aunt Willie told how men on their way to the sorghum mill would drive their wagons down the road past the Box Springs school. When the children were out at recess the men would usually stop and give them some stalks of sorghum cane to divide up. The boys would cut each stalk into several sticks and the children would peel them and eat them.

Shares—The sorghum mills, like other mills, are worked on shares or tolls and "No cash is exchanged in the deal." Mr. Edison Kilgore of Wing explained: "It is customary for the man who brings the cane to put it through the mill. He puts the juice into the pan." Also, "He furnishes the firewood." Then, "The man that's making it gets a third of

Everyone loves a sucker.

it." Farmer Wilhite recalled that his father usually planted enough cane so that he hoped to get three barrels of syrup. "One third to the mill man, one third for our use, and one third to sell. That was a cash crop."

Everyone looked forward to meeting at the sorghum mill. In the evening, after the molasses was made, there was usually a candy pulling. Patience demonstrated how to make molasses candy and explained as she did it: "You put molasses in the skillet and cook it till it was just real thick, you know, and then when it'd get cool we'd pull it and make candy out of it. It'd get hard and then we'd twist it, and then we'd let it get cool and we'd break it in sticks." She went on to say that it "takes four hands to pull. . . . Boys and girls would pull together."

Mrs. Hoggard recalled: "Lots of the young folks would get together and they'd make sorghum molasses candy. They'd boil the syrup down and before it got quite done they'd put a little soda in it and that'd make it foam up, you know, and get brittle. And then they'd take and pull that until it'd get just as white and bright." Lillie Sugg remembered that, "We'd pull candy and pull candy, and talk about a mess! The first thing you'd know he'd have it wrapped around your neck," and Polly said, "I pulled molasses candy till I had blisters on my hands."

When the candy-making was finished it was usually followed by a game called candy-breakin'. As Polly described it, "We broke this candy up in little pieces and we would have to put that little piece of candy in our mouth, and then our partner would bite the other end off. Wasn't that sneaky?" (Sometimes store-bought stick candy was used for this same game.)

Today sorghum-making is carefully regulated, and the neighborhood mills have almost gone the way of the local whiskey stills. However, processed sorghum can still be bought all over Arkansas, and many people who buy it as a curiosity wonder what to do with it when they get home. Here are some suggestions—serious and otherwise! It can be used in place of any other syrup on pancakes, biscuits, etc.; *or* you can mix it with your peas at suppertime, for as the song says, it makes the peas taste mighty funny, but it keeps them on your knife. You can do as the old man suggested and put it on your feet in the summer to keep the flies off your face *or* you can make this delicious sorghum cake:

Sorghum Cake (Gingerbread)

2 cups flour	⅓ cup butter
⅛ teaspoon soda	½ cup sugar

1 teaspoon cinnamon
½ teaspoon cloves
2 teaspoons ginger
1 teaspoon baking powder
½ teaspoon salt
1 egg
⅔ cup sorghum

¾ cup sour milk (To get your sour milk you can do as our grandmothers did and set a fruit jar with sweet milk in it on your doorstep in the sun—until the milk sours; or you can add a little less than 1 tablespoon vinegar to the sweet milk.)

Sift flour. Then measure and add your remaining dry ingredients and sift again. Cream the butter, add sugar and egg, and beat until light and fluffy. Add sorghum, then sour milk and dry ingredients. Mix well and pour into a well-greased and floured pan. Bake thirty minutes or more (depending on the size of your pan) at 350 degrees.

Quilting Bees

The names of quilt patterns tell us the story of pioneer life. The journey across the country is described in *Rocky-Road-to-California, Wagon Tracks, Texas Tears, Kansas Troubles, Arkansas Traveler, Trail-of-the-Covered-Wagon,* and *Indian Trails.* The life after they were settled is seen in *County Fair, Mill Wheel, Churn Dash, Rail Fence, Old Homestead, Log Cabin Star, Courthouse Square, Drunkard's Path, Goose-in-the-Pond,* and *Hole-in-the-Barn-Door.*

Today there are still women throughout the mountains making quilts in the same beautiful patterns that their great-grandmothers used so many years ago. Every scrap

A crazy quilt.

An appliqué quilt.

A patchwork quilt.

of cloth is used to make these colorful blankets, which not only keep the family warm and make the home more beautiful, but carry on a tradition that was practiced in Britain as early as the fourteenth century.

Quilting has always been a community affair and the quilting bee was another form of work that almost seemed like play. Once a woman had her quilt pieced and on the frame, the "neighbor women" all came in to help. A typical quilting party in the mountains was described by Aunt Chat: "We'd get a quilt up and ready. Then everybody in the country they'd meet. They'd put it up at a certain house and then we'd all go. And we'd quilt like nobody's business. Maybe we'd quilt two quilts or three quilts in one day, if they's enough a-women there. Why they'd just put it up—didn't have much houses—we could just put it up anywhere and just go to quiltin'. We used to use staple cotton and it beats this bought cotton a city block."

Patience remembered quilting bees as nighttime affairs, since the negro women had to work during the day. The whole family would come and "They'd make cake and stuff like that to pass around. You lived in a community— you put up a quilt and everybody'd go help you quilt it. The little children would thread the needles and hold the lamps—you had to have lamps to quilt by. The mens would be there too to help in the party. They'd make molasses candy and pull it. They'd be nice parties."

When a quilt was completed there was usually a traditional celebration. Patience recalled, "When they got the quilt made they used to 'christen' the quilt. They'd put a girl and a boy under it—the ones what was gonna marry soon."

Up in the Ouachitas Aunt Chat described another custom—one that is found throughout the Southern mountains. When the new quilt was taken off the frame, "Four of us would get ahold of the corners. And another one would have a cat. We'd begin to shake the quilt and they'd throw it [the cat] in, and the one it run out by was gonna get to marry first." When I asked her the name of this custom she said, "I don't remember of it being any special name but Shaking the Cat in the Quilt." Then I asked her if the cat ever ran out by her and she started laughing, "Oh, yes! I wouldn't shake too hard. I *wanted* it to come out by me!"

Roy Simpson gave a man's view of the same custom as he told about the time he taught at a country school and boarded with a family that had five unmarried daughters.

> The old custom was that you'd take a new quilt out of the frame and a girl would get at each corner. And you'd stick a cat in the middle of the quilt and toss the cat. And the one the cat ran out closest to would marry first.
>
> I remember one cool day there—and I very much looked in the fire while they were doing it—they got that new quilt out and got that cat and tossed it up and down in there till it ran out. But I think the cat got so scared it ran out by all of them—like jumping on a horse and riding off in all directions—because within a very short time they were all married.

Many people believed that whatever you dreamed the first night you slept under a new quilt would come true. So if the cat didn't run out by a girl she had a second chance if she dreamed of marrying her sweetheart.

Today, church groups, women's clubs, and farm wives are quilting all over Arkansas. But one of the most interesting tales concerns the ladies who sit quilting in the back room of an old store building in Leslie. The story begins many years ago when some of the small towns of Arkansas began slowly disappearing. These once-thriving communities faded away as the local mines closed, mills went out of business, railroads discontinued service, or the waters of artificial lakes covered them. In one town it got so bad that the county seat was moved and the courthouse was turned into a corncrib.

The ladies of Leslie and their "quilting commercial."

Leslie was one of these small villages nestled in the foothills of the Ozarks. To see the reason for its decline it is only necessary to look at the list of leading industries there during the early part of this century—a barrel factory, a hub mill that made wagonwheel hubs, a plant for making handles for plows, and a stave mill.

During the boom period of 1900 to 1940 the town supported four doctors; but as the industries died out and the shortage of rural doctors increased, Leslie found itself without any doctor at all. In the 1960's the people got together and decided to build a hospital to serve the surrounding area and to lure a physician back to Leslie.

Everyone began to work for the hospital. People contributed their time and talents, and at homecoming the ex-residents would donate money. The elderly ladies of the area felt that the main thing they could contribute was their talent for quilting. One by one, the women from the surrounding hills brought in squares of various quilt patterns as samples of their work. In the corner of each square they usually embroidered their name, and these were hung on the wall in the back room of a deserted store. In front of this "quilting commercial" a quilting frame was set up. When they had a chance the women would come in and work on the quilt that was in progress. As the quilts were sold the money was donated to the hospital fund.

Finally the hospital was built and was in operation, but the first doctor died and the second doctor quit and after a few years the hospital closed. But the ladies had formed the habit of coming in to quilt. And almost any weekday they can still be found in the back room of the store, quilting beside the old potbellied stove, remembering the times that have passed, and talking about the better days they hope are ahead.

PLAY PARTIES

On motion the following resolution was adopted: resolved that play parties should not be tolerated by the members of this church, resolved that Wee will not let such parties be given in our homes and that we will not go to them.

(Minutes, April, 1887, Big Creek Baptist Church)

In spite of the disapproval by some of the churches, the play party was a favorite diversion of the early Arkansas settlers. Originally the term "play party" was used to distinguish the gathering from a "dance," which was *forbidden* by most of the churches.

The differences were minor, but apparently they were important to churchgoing people. At play parties there was no instrumental music since fiddles and guitars were considered the instruments of the Devil. Instead, the music came from the singing, clapping, and foot-tapping of the participants. As one woman said, "Really it was dancing but you did it to singing." The emphasis at a play party was on games, and whole families attended rather than just courting couples. In fact some of the songs and games that our children know best, such as London Bridge, Jennie Crack Corn, and Drop the Handkerchief, were originally play-party games.

Invitations weren't issued, but as Vance Randolph said, word was "norated around." Sometimes they "blew up" the crowd by blowing on the party horn (as distinct from the church horn or the court horn). The best time to have a play party was right after a new house was built, before there was any furniture in it. If the house was already occupied, explained Farmer Wilhite, "They got the rooms cleared of the furniture. They had to take the beds down and take all the furniture out and set it on the porch or somewhere, 'cause the rooms were fairly small." In the summer the play party was sometimes held outside in the swept yard, preferably on a moonlit night, with pine knot torches for lights.

Mr. Simpson recalled that the country stumps "were usually done to a pine knot fire. Down there [in the Ouachitas] the pines very often became what we called 'rich'. The turpentine and tar in it made it what we called 'rich pine,' which is good for pine knot kindling and torches. A pine knot is made where the limb joined the trunk. It is kind of a beautiful thing . . . and they burn very readily."

Various people recalled games that were favorites in the old days but are not too well known today. Some of these are given below, with directions for the play in parentheses. Farmer Wilhite remembered the first three:

GREEN COFFEE GROWS

(They round up and then put two in the middle to start off. After that the song tells what to do.)

Green coffee grows on white oak tops,
The river flows with brandy, O.
Go choose you one to roam with you,
As sweet as 'lasses candy, O. (They choose a partner.)

Four in the middle and two on the side,
Four in the middle and two on the side,
Four in the middle and two on the side,
Swing four hands around you.

Swing by the right and by the left,
Swing by the right and by the left,
Swing by the right and by the left,
So early in the morning.

I sent my brown jug down to town,
I sent my brown jug down to town,
I sent my brown jug down to town,
So early in the morning.

It came back with a waltz-around,
It came back with a waltz-around,
It came back with a waltz-around,
So early in the morning.

GOING DOWN THE RIVER

(All of 'em that wants to get in the play, they circle up
holding hands. A boy and a girl get in the middle of the
ring. Then the rest ring up around them and they start.)

We're going down the river,
We're going down below,
We're going down the river,
To Old Shiloh.

Two in the ring and I can't dance, Josie,
Two in the ring and I can't dance, Josie,
Two in the ring and I can't dance, Josie,
Law, Susie Brown.

(During this, why, they're kinda making believe they're swinging.)

> Choose you'n a partner if you can't dance, Josie,
> Choose you'n a partner if you can't dance, Josie,
> Choose you'n a partner if you can't dance, Josie,
> Law, Susie Brown.

(When they each choose a partner, that makes four in the center.)

> Round up four if you can't dance, Josie,
> Round up four if you can't dance, Josie,
> Round up four if you can't dance, Josie,
> Law, Susie Brown.

> Right-left swing if you can't dance, Josie,
> Right-left swing if you can't dance, Josie,
> Right-left swing if you can't dance, Josie,
> Law, Susie Brown.

(There's any number of verses.)

> Hold my mule while I catch a possum,
> Hold my mule while I catch a possum,
> Hold my mule while I catch a possum,
> Law, Susie Brown.

> One wheel off the old brass wagon,
> One wheel off the old brass wagon,
> One wheel off the old brass wagon,
> Law, Susie Brown.

> Both wheels off and the axle draggin',
> Both wheels off and the axle draggin',
> Both wheels off and the axle draggin',
> Law, Susie Brown.

(The last verse was always):

> Get outta the ring if you can't dance, Josie,
> Get outta the ring if you can't dance, Josie,
> Get outta the ring if you can't dance, Josie,
> Law, Susie Brown.

(The first couple gets out, second couple stays in, and they do it all again.)

HOG DROVERS

(I guess you never heard of this—whether it was played anywhere but in Montgomery County I don't know.*

You take in the hills and in the mountains—the country people, they're all bashful. The boys are too bashful to ask a girl to be their partner and the girls, why, they wouldn't ask a boy to be their partner if they never had one. And so, a way to get 'em started off a girl and a boy, a girl and a boy—they'd get an older man—anybody thirty years old was an old man back in those days. They set down two chairs and he sits in one and they get some girl to come set down in the chair by the side of him. Then they all sing):

> Hog drovers,
> Hog drovers,
> Hog drovers we are.
> A-courting your daughter
> So rare and so fair.
> Can we get lodging here, oh, here?
> Can we get lodging here?

(Then the man sings):

This is my daughter that sets by my side,
And Mister_____(Calls boy's name) can make her his bride,
If he'll bring me another one here, oh, here,
If he'll bring me another one here.

*It was. See "Swine-herders" in Newell's *Games and Songs of American Children*. (Dover)

(The boy named gets that girl for his partner and he brings another girl to set down there and they go on until they're all partnered up.)

Another old game that also uses two chairs is one remembered by Patience. She said, "We used to play Scornin' Plays"; and explained how you put the two chairs together—side by side—one facing one way and one facing the other. A girl sits in one chair looking straight

Patience shows Lee and Russ how to play Scorn.

ahead and a boy comes up, sits down in the other chair, and tries to kiss her. If the girl doesn't want the boy to kiss her she turns away (scorns him), and another boy comes. When she lets a boy kiss her she leaves and another girl comes and sits down. Or as Patience said (to the boy), "You make like you gonna kiss her and she turn her head—she scorn you"; and (to the girl), "You turn your head right quick—scorn him." Then she explained, "He set down and she turn her head from him—don't kiss him. When she scorn him somebody else get up and get in this chair. And if she like him—she kiss him."

Newell described a similar game played in New England and also called Scorn. He explained:

> A girl was seated on a chair in the middle of the room, and one child after another was led to her throne. She would turn away with an expression of contempt, until some one approached that pleased her, who, after a kiss, took her place.
>
> Derision is the name of a game mentioned by Froissart as an amusement of his childhood. It is not at all unlikely that the present sport represents the old French pastime.

How the game got from France to the plantation country of Arkansas remains a mystery.

Another "pairing-up" game in the black community was called Walking on the Green Grass and was taught to me by Louise Parsons:

> (The boys and girls line up in two lines; just say eight over here and eight over here—or just three or four can play it. Well, you just walk up and down, between the two lines, singing):
>
>> Walking on the green grass,
>> Me and two, three more.
>> My foot slipped
>> And I fell down,
>> And I was 'shamed to go.

Court the girl with the coal black hair,
Court the girl with the money,
Court the girl with the coal black hair,
Me and two, three more.

(Then a boy picks a girl and they walk up and down between the lines till they get through singing that. Then they stand aside and another one goes.)

The one game mentioned by the most people was Skip to My Lou. This was primarily a game of "stealing partners," which Patience described as, "Me and my boyfriend, we's standin' together; you and your boyfriend; her and her boyfriend. My boyfriend go and steal you—take you by the arm and go to another place. Then your partner go steal him another girl."

Here are some of the many verses mentioned by various people:

SKIP TO MY LOU

(Partners all around—extra boy in the middle.)

Skip, skip, skip to my Lou,
Skip, skip, skip to my Lou,
Skip, skip, skip to my Lou,
Skip to my Lou, my darlin'.

Stole my partner and what'll I do? etc.

Get me another'n that's what I'll do, etc.
   (or)
I'll get another'n prettier'n you, etc.

Pretty as a redbird, prettier too, etc.

Flies in the buttermilk—shoo, fly, shoo, etc.

Chicken in the breadpan pickin' out dough, etc.

Little red wagon painted blue, etc.

Gone again, what'll I do? etc.

Another old song, remembered by Granny Riddle, also was played in a circle.

GREEN GRAVEL

Green gravel, green gravel,
The grass is so green.
There's a pretty, fair maiden,
Ashamed* to be seen.
Oh _____, Oh _____ (Call one of the girls' names),
Your true lover is dead.
He writ you a letter,
Now turn your head.
(The girl whose name is called turns and they sing to the next one.)

John Gideon remembered this game that came from Ireland and was especially popular in the South:

KING WILLIAM WAS KING JAMES' SON

King William was King James' son,
Upon a royal race he run.
Upon his breast he wore a star.
(Points to the Eastern Star)
Go East, go West,
And choose the one
You love the best.
If she's not here to take your part,
Choose another with all your heart.
Down on this carpet you must kneel
As sure as the grass grows in the field.
Salute your bride and kiss her sweet
And now you rise upon your feet.

*Some folklorists feel that "ashamed" was originally "arrayed."

We were at Aunt Willie's eighty-fifth birthday party
when Aunt Edna (age eighty-nine) sang the following song
for me. On the second verse she jumped up and stuck out
her arms. When I asked her what on earth she was doing,
she said, "I'm measuring my love!" Here is the game:

WE'RE MARCHING ROUND THE LEVEE*

> We're marching round the levee,
> We're marching round the levee,
> We're marching round the levee,
> And hope to gain the day.

(A whole group marches side by side—in partners.)

> I'll measure my love to show you,
> I'll measure my love to show you,
> I'll measure my love to show you,
> For we have gained this day.

(You line up in two lines and turn toward each other. Then
you hold your arms out to "measure your love—by the
yard.")

> Go forth and choose your lover,
> Go forth and choose your lover,
> Go forth and choose your lover,
> For we have gained this day.

(One goes *forth*—back in line—and the other one skips
down to the end and gets a new partner.)

Roy Simpson gave the words and directions for a similar
game:

---

*In *American Folk Tales and Songs*, Richard Chase says, "'Levee' here has no connection
with flood control! It must mean a morning party or reception. Such levees were held
during the War Between the States to celebrate victories . . . 'For we have gained the
day.'"

(The circle formed and all but one player joined hands in a circle. The first stanza went:)

> Go in and out the windows,
> Go in and out the windows,
> Go in and out the windows,
> And I hope we gain today.

(The arms, hands joined, were raised to permit the lone player in the circle to go in and out, circling the players one by one as he did.)

> Go forth and face your lover,
> Go forth and face your lover,
> Go forth and face your lover,
> And I hope we gain today.

(The boy went over and led one of the girls to the center of the ring.)

> I measure my love to show you,
> I measure my love to show you,
> I measure my love to show you,
> And I hope we gain today.

(Here the two in the ring joined their hands and stretched their arms out horizontally in a measuring motion.)

> I kneel because I love you,
> I kneel because I love you,
> I kneel because I love you,
> And I hope we gain today.

(Here the boy, holding only one hand now, kneels before his love in deep devotion.)

> One sweet kiss and I must leave you,
> One sweet kiss and I must leave you,
> One sweet kiss and I must leave you,
> And I hope we gain today.

(This verse we usually omitted, but once when I was in the ring, it was sung. I moved toward my partner to execute what was demanded. [He and his partner, Nellie, were both thirteen.] I have known for well over sixty years that the stiff-arm was not invented by football backs, for Nellie stiff-armed me as effectively as any ball carrier could— there beneath the summer sun.)

> Good-bye, I hate to leave you,
> Good-bye, I hate to leave you,
> Good-bye, I hate to leave you,
> And I hope we gain today.

(As this stanza was sung, the boy dropped back into line, leaving the girl to make the next choice as the verses were repeated.)

When the play party was over, the pioneers could close the evening by all joining hands to play Shoot the Buffalo; with its appropriate verse:

> Rise ye up, my dearest dear,
> Present me to your pa,
> And we'll all march together,
> To the state of Arkansas.

SQUARE DANCES AND HOEDOWNS

> Had a gal, her name was Sal,
> Down in Arkansas.
> Loved her once and I love her still,
> Down in Arkansas.
> Down in Ark-an,
> Down in Ark-an,
> Down in Arkansas.
> The only gal I ever loved, lived—
>   "Granny, will your dog bite?"
>   "No, child, no!"
> Down in Arkansas.

For the braver souls, hoedowns and square dances were the favorite forms of musical get-togethers. Both were in disfavor with the church for a long time because of the musical instruments that were used (and the jug of corn squeezings that were present), but both found favor with the fun-loving folks of the mountains. Roy Simpson told about the time he "stood by the superintendent of the Sunday School at Cherry Hill, while we listened to the fiddler for a medicine show that came through; and the superintendent said he thought the devil was in the fiddle." However, Mr. Simpson went on to say that, "In spite of all that, I heard a great deal of fiddling."

In fact, it was customary for some people to succumb to the lure of dancing on long winter evenings and be expelled from the church; then repent and be readmitted at the camp meeting the next summer. This would go on year after year!

Traveling through the hills today you might hear someone call out "Green Corn," "Leather Britches" (beans), "Possum Sop and Polecat Gravy," or "Bile Them Cabbage Down," and expect to catch a whiff of country cooking soon. But these are just some of the colorful names for the songs that the local musicians love to play. Most of these tunes have been handed down from generation to generation and many of the songs can be traced back to the beginnings of our nation's history and even beyond to the early ballads of Scotland and England. Sometimes even the rollicking old church songs were given secular words and became "folly ballads" or "giddy tunes." As Aunt Chat said about one of her favorites, "It was a hymnal song, but Pa changed the words up."

In the old days (as today) when the music got lively the dancing began. One of the favorite forms was the square dance with four couples in a fast-running set. Each square dance consisted of established patterns shouted out by a caller. My father-in-law recalled that "Sometimes the one that would pick the banjo would call, and a lot of times the

Seth Mize with his fiddle.

caller would be in the square—he'd be dancing and calling."

When the caller began tapping his foot and shouting out the do-si-do's it was hard to resist the lure. Especially with such exciting dance names as: Chase the Goose, Shoot the Owl, Break the Chicken's Neck, Roll the Barrel, Dive and Shoot the Turkey Buzzard, Shuck the Corn, Unwind the Yarn, Weave the Basket, Dig for the Oyster, or Take a Peek.

The dances lasted most of the night and Ed Ballentine said his father "could play the fiddle from night till morning and never repeat a tune." John Gideon recalled,

"We rode eight or ten miles horseback to attend a square dance and the poor old mule or horse waited out in cold, rain, or snow until wee hours of morn to take us home." Roy Simpson said that around his home, "Feet Davis and Marvin furnished the fiddling. Ordinarily they got their pay by charging say ten or fifteen cents 'on the corner', they called it, for each dance. The man paid the fiddler and the old expression, 'You must pay the fiddler,' might have come from that."

To keep the music flowing the fiddler often needed a drink for stamina or encouragement. One man said, "We always had to have our little bit of moonshine—we'd whoop it up. It'd be in those quart fruit jars just as clear as water." Gerstaeker described an Arkansas square dance he attended, where the first fiddler finished up his part of the evening with

> a few impulsive draws of the bow, which caused the fiddle to squeak wildly. Now rolling his eyes he began to condemn the whole party in no uncertain terms. (He had finished two bottles of whiskey.) He began to cry, and without any ado four young men picked him up and carried him out. This little intermezzo naturally interrupted the dance. Another man volunteered to find a sober fiddler. To bridge the intermission a young man rolled up his sleeves and started to beat his open hands rhythmically upon his knees. In two minutes the dance was in full sway again.
>
> At last the promised musician arrived but not in the expected condition; he too was not entirely sober. As one man remarked in a knowing manner, "he would do until midnight." . . . Shortly after twelve o'clock the prophecy of our friend came true, and our second fiddler was carried out and laid on the grass to sleep away his intoxication. A third took his place.

Such was the state of Arkansas fiddlers in the early 1800's. For a complete square dance, here is one from the early 1900's, as recalled by Farmer Wilhite:

Come and go,
Bring and fetch,
Ring and twist.
Catch your partner by the craw
And swing around old Arkansas.

Let's have four couples on the floor
We'll dance this set and forty more.
Partners to your places
And straighten up your faces,
Gather up the lines and tighten up the traces.

Join hands and circle eight.

Right foot up and the left foot down,
Make that big foot jar the ground.
Turn right back, you're goin' wrong,
But keep that rhythm goin' on.

And stop at home.
And ladies whirl,
And gents whirl,
And everybody whirl.

Round up eight and all get straight.

Now first get out—number one.
Swing your right-hand lady with a right-hand swing,
Swing your left-hand lady with a left-hand swing,
Opposite lady with a two-hand swing.
Partner to the center and seven in the ring.

Eight hands up and gone again.
Balance one, balance all,
Swing your opposite across the hall.
Swing 'em on the corner as you come down
Back to your partner and promenade around.

Round up eight and all get straight.
Stop at home.

Having fun with their music! Bookmiller Shannon is picking his own banjo and fingering Lonnie Avey's guitar. Lonnie is picking his own guitar and fingering Bookmiller's banjo.

First couple out—number one pick up number two.

Lady round the lady with the gents so low,
Lady round the gent, but the gent don't go.

Round up four in the middle of the floor.
Right hands crossed.
Left back.

Join your right and seesaw back,
Do-si-do,
Gents you know,
You know how to make a cornbread dough.

Chicken in the breadpan peckin' out dough,
Granny, will the dog bite?
No, child, no.

Round up four and pick up three.

Break and walk that tater vine walk.
First around the lady and then around the gent.

And round up six and all get fixed.
Right hands crossed—form a star.
Left hands back
Join your right and seesaw back.
Do-si-do.

Courtship and Marriage

Roxie Ann's a pretty little girl
I knowed it all the while.
She's been a long time foolin', foolin',
She's been a long time foolin' me.

Fool 'em, Roxie, fool 'em.
Fool 'em if you can.
She's been a long time foolin', foolin',
She's been a long time foolin' me.
                                    (Old Play-Party Song)

All the play parties, square dances, candy-pullings, and "bees" gave young couples a chance to meet, and naturally courtships began. First came the "settin'-up" period, when the boys came to call and set up with the girl.* Some people remembered the boys settin' up all night, but Patience recalled, "When the boys set up with us—old

---

*In *Down in the Holler*, Vance Randolph and George Wilson define "Set up to" as "*v.i.* To woo, to court. 'Jake he's *a-settin'* up to a gal over on Gander Mountain.'"

folks wouldn't let 'em stay except till nine o'clock. Nine o'clock come—they knew to go home." And, "They didn't 'low 'em to come but once a week."

Farmer Wilhite remembered a more tiresome kind of settin' up as it was practiced in the mountains: "Here's a girl that was pretty popular and there was more than one boy that would like to, as they say, 'set up' with her. When they were goin' a-courtin' 'they called it 'settin' up' with 'em. They were liable to be there by breakfast time on Sunday." One boy would come, then another, then maybe a third would come. Nobody would leave. "They'd stay for dinner and stay for supper." Then, "by-doggies, nobody was gonna be the first one to leave a-tall and they'd just stay and set up all night.

"There's an old, old song that really comes from away back, 'Hard is the Fortune'—that really tells it":

Hard is the fortune of all womankind
Always controll-ed and always confined.
Controlled by their parents until they're made wives,
Then they're enslaved for the rest of their lives.

Young men they'll go courting all dressed out so fine;
To fool these poor girls, they will say she's divine.
They'll hug and they'll kiss them until they're made wives.
Then they're enslaved for the rest of their lives.

The girls get so tired, they rise up and say,
"Oh, boys, I'm so sleepy, I wish you'd go 'way."
"Go away from you, darling," they answer in scorn,
"Before I will leave, I'll go sleep in your barn."

Then early next morning so early they rise,
Brush the hay from their clothes and the sleep from their eyes.
They'll saddle their horses and away they will ride,
These false-hearted lovers their faces to hide.

194 GARDEN SASS

The girls they did up with a stagger and reel,
God bless these poor girls, how tired they do feel.
If I were a young man I'd court none at all
I'd stay single at home and I'd keep the bachelor's hall.

For bach-e-lors hall I'm convinced is the best,
Go drunk or go sober, go home to your rest.
No wife there to scold you, no babies to squall,
And happy is the man who keeps bach-e-lor's hall.

For the boys who did not keep bachelor's hall a wedding soon followed the "settin'-up" period. Often the marriage was performed at the home of the bride or of some close relative who had a house large enough. After the wedding there was usually a big infare party for everyone, with a banquet and dancing.

An early wedding banquet (1857) was described by an old man in the book, *History of Lawrence, Jackson, Independence and Stone Counties, Arkansas:* "When anybody married, then they had a regular jubilee, danced all night and all day. The wedding tables were ornamented with cakes and butter strained through a coarse cloth to resemble fountains, water falls, and moulded in the hands into ducks with bead eyes, or with a spoon into pine burrs." After the wedding dinner the couple settled down with the bride's parents, to stay anywhere from "one to two days" to "forever."

Even before the white man came, the Indians of Arkansas were celebrating weddings. A description of a Cherokee wedding was given to Cephas Washburn by one of his Indian friends named Blanket. Originally Washburn found Blanket living with a sister, who was a widow, and later, with a niece. When he asked Blanket if he had not been married the answer was, "Yes, once, but my wife was a singing bird and we divided the blankets." This unusual expression, indicating divorce, was made clear as Washburn learned of the Indian wedding ceremony:

Blanket gave me an account of the ancient custom of his people in solemnizing the rite of marriage. The preliminaries were settled by the mother and one of her brothers on both sides. Generally the parties themselves had formed a previous attachment, and made request of these relatives that they might be married; but it was also often the case that the groom and bride were not consulted at all until the actual solemnization was appointed. But to the ceremony itself. The whole town were convened, all attired in their gravest apparel. The groom accompanied by the young associates of his own sex was feasted in a lodge at a little distance from the council-house. The bride, with her maiden associates, was similarly feasted in a lodge equi-distant from the council-house and on the opposite side. First the old men took the highest seats on one side of the council-house, next the old women took similar seats on the other side. Then all the married men took seats on the side occupied by the old men, and all the married women sat on the side with the old women. At a given signal, the companions of the groom conducted him to the open end of the open space between the women and men in the council-house. The companions of the bride conduct her to the other end of this open space, and they now stand with their faces towards each other, about at a distance of from thirty to sixty feet apart, according to the size of the council-house. The groom now receives from his mother a leg of venison and a blanket; the bride receives from her mother an ear of corn and a blanket. The groom and the bride now commence stepping towards each other, and when they meet in the middle of the council-house the groom presents his venison, and the bride her corn, and the blankets are united. This ceremony put into words is a promise on the part of the man that he will provide meat for his family, and on the woman's part that she will furnish bread, and on the part of both that they will occupy the same bed.

After this, holding each to an end of the united blankets, and the husband holding the corn and the wife the venison, they walk along silently to a new cabin which is to be their future home. It is on account of this ceremony that separation of husband and wife, is expressed by the significant terms, "Dividing the blankets."

SHIVAREES

Charivari (Fr.)—a mock serenade made by blowing toy horns, beating on pans, etc.; often played as a practical joke on newly married couples.

(*Webster's New World Dictionary*)

One of the favorite get-togethers of mountain people took place after the wedding party. This was the charivari, or as it became known in America, the shivaree. Few people today even recognize the word "shivaree"; but in some places in the Ozark mountains the ceremony is still used to welcome a newly married couple to the community.

The shivaree began in the Middle Ages and there are many variations on the way it is conducted. Throughout the mountains there is a typical form that has been used for generations. All of the friends of a newly married couple gather together on the wedding night and march to the home where the couple is staying. When they reach the house a noisy demonstration begins, with shotguns blasting, bells ringing, and pots and pans being beaten. They march around and around the house, being joined by the howling of the dogs and the "pot-breaking" of the chickens.

Sim Goodman described a typical shivaree in Grant County:

Every time a couple got married, why we had a "shivaree" we called it—we'd serenade 'em. Get together and we'd have a lot of cowbells and—we had no band or anything—but if somebody had a fiddle they'd play the fiddle and guitar and we'd shoot guns and ring the bells and sing and holler and whoop it up. Till finally somebody'd come to the door and they'd invite us in and have a cake or somethin'—most of the time it was some corn liquor. When some couple got married we'd always give them a big shivaree.

Uncle Sam Hess, ninety-two, plays the same banjo he played on the night he was shivareed—in the same house.

When I asked Aunt Chat if she was shivareed she shouted, "Wowee, yes! That was the fun there was to it. They jarred everything off of the ground. They shot guns, they rung bells, they beat plows—and got ahold of an old circle saw and they'd put a pole in the center, and one get on each side to carry it, you know, and people'd walk behind and beat on this old circle saw."

Farmer Wilhite also remembered how they would beat on a circular saw at a shivaree, and explained how they would blow on a wagon skein. They would take an old skein, "one that's worn out so it's no good to the wagon, 'n they'd knock that off the axle. And man, that makes the darndest horn to blow. It'll jar ya in your chair." He also recalled that "depending if anybody had any money, they'd get a keg of powder and they'd get a couple of anvils and shoot the anvils . . . . They'd shoot anvils then till they used up that keg of powder."

The horseplay and noise continued until the newlyweds finally came to the door. When the door opened, the crowd marched in the front and out the back making music and noise the whole time. Granny Riddle remembered that in her community there was always someone with a hunting horn leading the crowd in and out.

After enough noise had been made, the unhappy groom was grabbed by the crowd and often tied to a rail (hence the term "ridden on a rail") and carried to the nearest creek where he was dumped into the icy water. Colonel Buxton recalled the time when they "put the couple in a steel wheelbarrow and rolled them right down Main Street." There was never any pleasure in this part of the shivaree, but not to be shivareed was a terrible fate in a community where it was the custom. In fact, the number of people at the "belling" and the enthusiasm of the crowd was a good indication of the couple's popularity.

After this part of the shivaree was over, the bride and groom were expected to "stand for treats." This could be as simple as handing a five-dollar bill to the leader of the group and telling him to take everyone to the local store and buy them some candy and cigars. But a good-natured couple would usually invite the crowd in for refreshments. In the old days this led to a party with singing and games, pies and cakes, and sometimes corn liquor made just for the occasion.

When the couple finally said good-bye to the last of the crowd they usually had one more indignity to suffer. One woman recalled that "if they possibly could—if the family was in on it—why, they'd fix the slats so they'd break—so the bed would fall down."

Despite the fact that it sounds so gruesome, people enjoy talking about their own shivaree or the ones they've attended. Uncle Sam Hess, age ninety-two, sat down and played the same songs on the same old banjo that he played for the crowd on the night he and his wife Emma were shivareed at her father's home.

Kermit Moody remembered the time he attended a shivaree that became an excuse for "shooting up the town." Many years ago in Stone County this group of young men on their way to a shivaree began shooting off their guns in the middle of Mountain View. Afterward they rushed into a nearby restaurant and hid their guns under the mattress of a bed that was kept in a back room of the cafe. When they went back outside the sheriff and his deputy were rushing down the street looking for the people who had done the shooting. The boys kindly offered to help in the search and soon had the sheriff going in circles. First they would report that someone had seen the men with the guns down at the blacksmith shop and the sheriff would rush off in that direction; then the pranksters would hurry down to tell him that some men with guns had just been spotted going down another street and the sheriff would rush to check on that. Finally the boys gathered up their guns and went on to the shivaree, leaving the sheriff to search without their "help."

For bashful bridal couples there was often a battle of wits as they tried to elude the merrymakers. Farmer explained that whenever possible the bridal couple would disguise themselves in some garb during the infare party and escape before the shivaree began. He laughed as he said, "I've been to some shivarees when it turned out that the bride and groom wasn't there a-tall."

Today there are fewer and fewer shivarees and the

custom is fast dying out. But up in the Ozarks you may still run into a man who will recall, as he lights a cigar, that at so-and-so's shivaree the groom passed out cigars to about forty men who all smoked them in that one room, making all the women sick, and "my wife could never stand cigar smoke after that shivaree." However, now more of the young people are tying tin cans on the cars and writing messages on the car windows of their newly married friends—techniques that may be almost as frustrating but probably not half as much fun as a full-fledged shivaree.

Tick-Tacking

Tick-tacking was another form of harassment, but one that could be practiced on anybody at any time. In the *History of Ashley County* the author describes a shivaree as "making music, singing, tick-tacking the bridal chamber . . . and general whoop-them-up conduct." Bessie Wilhite also remembered tick-tacking as being part of the shivaree. But her husband said, "Aw, shucks, they wouldn't pay no more attention to that at a shivaree than a mosquito a-buzzin'!"

Anyway, whether it was used on a bridal couple or on "just anybody to have some fun out of," the mountaineers loved to tease each other with the ghostly sounds of a tick-tack. Farmer Wilhite describes how it was done in the Ouachita Mountains:

> You first take a good strong sliver of hardwood and trim it down very thin so's it'll stick into a crack or under a siding board or any place around. And you take a coarse thread and you tie it to this little splinter. And then you've got to slip up—you see, the family there's got to know nothin' about anybody bein' anywhere around. And you get up and find a place to stick this splinter in under a window casing, or anywhere you can to stick it in there. And then he lets this spool of thread unwind and he gets out there

behind some bushes or behind the smokehouse or someplace and he pulls it tight. And he has some pine resin or beeswax on his fingers and he pulls it and he runs his hand up and down that string—and the tighter he pulls why the higher it goes. It goes *whoooooo-eeeeeeee-eeee.*

They try to stick the splinter up as high as they can so if anybody comes around the house, you see, it'll be plumb up above their heads. And if they come out why you let up on it. Then when they go back in the house why they pull that string tight and theygo *zzzzzzzzzz-eeeeeeee.* Then when they get about to be caught up with, why they just break the thread off and they hull out.

A lonely house was the perfect place for tick-tacking.

Aunt Willie told about the time this was pulled on her parents (in the Ozarks):

Isaac Harkey was our nextdoor neighbor—he was on the next farm—and he studied pranks and jokes all his life.

And my father always hated to get out in the cold in the wintertime. But one night—way in the night—they heard this sawin' and buzzin' and my father woke my mother up and she heard it, and she listened to it, and it just kept on till they couldn't stand it anymore. And it was a real cold night! So, my father got up and got on his clothes and got out there and looked all around. And it hushed—just hushed completely—couldn't hear a sound. And he went back to bed and hadn't much more than got warm and it started again. So he got up that time and he took the hammer with him—and he knocked and hammered and he pulled the plank off that the nail was fastened in. Well, of course it completely stopped for a good long time. But then a third time it happened! And they didn't know for a good long time what had happened . . . . They called it tick-tacking.

CHAPTER 6
MAKE AND MAKE DO

The homemade sign by the beaver dam says, PLEAS DO NOT KILL THE BEAVERS—WE WANT THE POND FER STOCK WATER. It was put there by a ninety-year-old farmer, and typifies the hillman's ability to make use of whatever nature provides.

From their thrifty Scotch ancestors the people of Arkansas learned to either make the things they needed or make do with the things they had. What nature didn't provide, the early settlers had to make for themselves, including such makeshifts as shoestrings from groundhog hides, jelly from corncobs, syrup from hickory bark, and hair dye from potato peelings. As Farmer Wilhite said: "You take people livin' on a homestead out in the woods—why, there wasn't a store right across the road to go and get whatever you need. And so if you needed somethin' why you went and made it. And with might near no tools to work with!" Or, as Lonzo Tallent put it, "Today they have these conveniences that they make for everything, but in the old days there weren't any." To make up for his lack of "conveniences" the Arkansas settler fell back on a number of ingenious folkways, most of them very old in origin.

*The pioneer spirit: When one part
wears out—substitute another.*

SLEDGES

When he first arrived in the Ozarks the pioneer was
often confronted with a piece of land completely covered
with rocks. To clear his fields he set to work making one of
the oldest vehicles known to mankind, a wooden sledge.
This was a practice that came down from the earliest times
and was brought over by the first settlers on their voyage
from the British Isles. As Kevin Danaher explained the
origin of this idea: "It is not easy to drag a load over rough
ground, and even on smooth ground the load may suffer.
But a good leafy branch can be piled with firewood or hay
or the carcass of a deer and hauled along by the stem.
Once that step was thought out it required only a little
imagination to produce a rudimentary sledge, and many
sledges still have the triangular form of the tree branch.

But the simple sledge on two runners is the commonest form." (*In Ireland Long Ago*)

Uncle Sam Hess has an ancient sledge that was used in clearing the rocks from his farm. He explained the advantages of a sled over a wagon: A sled was less strenuous to load because the rocks didn't have to be lifted

An Ozark sled.

up so high; it was easier for a team of oxen to pull; and it was less likely to tip over on rough ground. Also, it was simpler to build.

After the fields were cleared the sled was used to take hay down into the back pastures, to remove dead cattle, or

to transport anything that was heavy around the farm. A
sled was almost a necessity of life, and Roy Simpson told
how the untitled "squatters'" farms "were occasionally sold
for a pocketknife or a sled. I have known of such
transactions."

Today farmers still use these old sleds behind their
tractors to haul apples, peaches, and other produce out of
the orchards. They usually call them "sleds," although
some people make the distinction that sleds were used only
in winter and sledges were used the year around.

BROOMS

There has been a need for a broom as long as there has
been someone to insist on cleanliness, and the pioneer
homestead was no exception. Even the yards were swept
clean of every bit of trash, grass, animal droppings, etc.
Aunt Willie recalled, "Sweeping the yard—that was
instead of mowing like folks do today. Why, the cleaner
your yard the better. You didn't want one weed or a blade
of grass or anything on it. But you had to sweep the yards
every week—that was something that *had* tc be done. And
they had to be absolutely clean of all rubbish or sticks or
anything."

Roy Simpson said, "I never saw any country yard that
had a lawn. They'd take an old brush broom or one made
out of cane and get out and sweep it." Aunt Alma recalled
that she used dogwood branches tied together to make a
yard broom when she was a girl. It was her job to sweep
the yard every Saturday because her family lived near the
church, and on Sundays the preacher usually came home
to dinner with them.

Inside the house there were several types of brooms that
were used. One was the old brush broom like the ones
made by the "broom-squires" in England. A large handful
of straw, preferably broom straw, was bound together

around a strong stick, making a flat or round broom similar to the ones we use today. John Gideon claimed he "made our broom out of a hoe handle and buck brush."

A popular type of broom used in the early days was the cornshuck mop. Aunt Willie told how one of these was made and used:

> We got a thick piece of board and took it to my grandfather's shop and made holes with an auger. Then we took the shucks and dampened 'em till they would be real easy to twist up. And we twisted 'em and poked 'em through the holes in the board and left enough on the outside to scrub the floors . . . .
>
> We would go to our grandmother's in Belleville, and when we started back up the mountain the horse would always balk. We always had a balky horse! So when we'd start up the mountain my father'd stop the wagon and we'd all get out to walk except him. The horse would go on if there wasn't anybody in there. And as we went up the mountain we'd pick up pieces of white sandstone. And when we'd get home and start to do housecleaning—we'd take that sandstone and take a hammer and it would just crumble up and be the prettiest, whitest sand. You sprinkled it on the floor with lye soapsuds and scrubbed the floors till they would be just as white as could be. Of course you did all of this with a shuck mop.

A cornshuck mop.

Another man explained how useful a shuck broom could be. "On summer afternoons Mama sat on the porch shelling her peas or peeling her apples, and the children joined her with cookies or cake in their hands. Soon the chickens were on the porch pecking around at the cookie crumbs, stray peas, or apple peelings, and leaving their drippings behind. That is where the cornshuck broom came in handy. At the end of the day water was poured on the porch and the rough old cornshuck broom gave it a good scrubdown. When the shucks were worn out one of the kids was sent to the corncrib to get some more to replace them."

BEDDING

Go tell Aunt Rhody,
Go tell Aunt Rhody,
Go tell Aunt Rhody,
The old grey goose is
    dead.

The one that she's been
    savin',
The one that she's been
    savin',
The one that she's been
    savin',
To stuff her feather bed.
(Old Lullaby)

Nowhere did the settler's wife use more ingenuity than she did in providing bedding for her family. Quilts, shuck mattresses, and feather beds were made by the thrifty farm wife from things that we would call castoffs.

In an old song, a man looks back on his life with regret and admits that "If I had listened to what Mama said, I'd be sleepin' on a feather bed." To provide this comfortable bedding, most farmhouses had a flock of geese that were well cared for even though they were a lot of trouble. It is easy to see where the expression "silly as a goose" comes from, when you hear Aunt Willie explain, "When it rained the geese would just stand there with their heads up—and stand there and drown. So when it started raining you had to get up and get the geese in."

The first step in making the feather bed was to pluck the geese, for as another old saying goes, "Them that don't pluck don't get no feathers." According to the superstitious this had to be done on a new moon, but according to Aunt Willie, "You just had to wait till their feathers were ripe or it would hurt them so bad."

The directions for making a feather bed are given by Granny Riddle:

> Get ticking—and just sew it up as wide as you want your bed—and then make another one the same width. Now don't get it too big or it'll hang off the sides. You want a feather bed to stay well inside your mattress. But make it where it comes plumb out to the edge and a little bit over.
>
> And then to box the corners you just simply sew crossways and that boxes the corners. Leave a place either in the end or to the middle—wherever you want to—and just shake out feathers in there until you get, oh, as much as ten or fifteen pounds in if you want a good heavy one.
>
> They raised geese and ducks and you pluck them twice a year. You don't take these wing feathers. But on the breast, all through the breast, the downy feathers—you pick them. You pluck those feathers that are ripe. You have to wait till a certain time and when they get fully feathered they'll shed them off, if you don't pluck them off. You pick them off in the spring and fall, and as you pick them you put them in a bag. But you sun those feathers till they're dry, and then you put them in your bed. They call them green feathers if you don't sun them, and they get smelly.

Underneath the feather bed, and on top of the rope

slats, was the cornshuck mattress. This was made like the feather bed, but with a filling of dried cornshucks, straw, grass, or even Spanish moss. According to Farmer Wilhite there were some disadvantages to each of these sturdy mattresses. He recalled that:

Grass or straw—"It'll get packed down to where it's just as hard as a floor. You've got to take and get some new grass and put in it, or fluff this up. We didn't fluff 'em up ever time we made the bed up. But ever week or so, why, you'd take the broom handle and you'd just whack that—whack, whack, whack. And that fluffs it up and makes it a whole lot softer."

Cornshuck—"You take your corn, where you've shucked your corn, and you've got to strip these shucks all up fine. But that's the noisiest thing to sleep on. Ever time you move—you just wiggle your toe—and rattle, rattle, rattle." (John Gideon recalled that every spring they shredded fresh cornshucks to make their ticks and "These had to be worked over every few weeks.")

Spanish moss—In southern Arkansas they filled their mattresses with Spanish moss that they harvested from the trees in boats, and "That makes a whole lot better bed tick than grass," but was harder to get.

Perhaps the ultimate in comfort was the bed described by the braggart who resided in the town of Shirt-tail Bend, Arkansas (in the book *The Big Bear of Arkansas,* written by T. B. Thorpe in 1846). He urged a stranger to come stay with him for "a month or a year" and promised: "I can give you plenty to eat, for besides hog and hominy, you can have b'ar-ham, and b'ar sausages, and a mattress of b'ar-skins to sleep on, and a wildcat skin, pulled off hull, stuffed with cornshucks, for a pillow. That bed would put you to sleep if you had the rheumatics in every joint in your body. I call that ar bed a *quietus.*"

CONTAINERS

Baskets, gums, and gourds were the three types of containers that every family on the frontier could get for themselves. To obtain crocks, tinware, or iron pots they were usually dependent on the peddler, but baskets they could make, gums they could find, and gourds they could grow.

Almost every settlement had someone who could make baskets out of white oak or hickory splits or cornshucks. For the box suppers at school John Gideon even recalled how the girls would make corn *stalk* baskets in the shape of a log cabin. In addition, many enterprising pioneers wove baskets from the long pine-needles that covered the ground. One who does this today is Rosie McKay, who

Rosie McKay sits out under the trees making her pine-needle baskets.

chooses loblolly pine needles about ten inches long "that come from down at Camden," or longer ones from other places when she can get them. To prepare the needles, she explains, "You just pour boiling water on 'em for about five or ten minutes. That makes 'em soft. You wrap 'em in a towel and they'll stay damp from one day to the next."

To sew the needles together she uses "real stout raffia" that she orders from the "place where I get my seeds in the spring." Taking a few needles at a time, she bends them and sews them together with various stitches. "This outside stitch—this is called the wheat stitch—where there's one on each side. And I think this is the briar stitch. The fern stitch—that's just whipped around. And I just make up my own designs." When she is finished she has an unusual little basket that can be used for a number of purposes.

The hollow gum-trees made useful containers for larger items. Some of the gums were split sideways to make large

A gum used as a salt lick on the side of a log cabin.

feeding or watering troughs for livestock and to make troughs to hold the salted meat during hog-killing time. Others were left upright, and as Gerstaeker noted, "These gums serve many purposes; often they are used as bee-gums; in houses they serve as bins in which cornmeal and salt are kept."

But the most useful containers of all were the gourds. Around the chicken house the pioneer planted his gourd vines to help keep the mites away and to provide him with gourds for dozens of uses. There were gourds of every size and shape and most of them had their own name and particular purpose.

To begin with, there was a *bottle* gourd, often filled with whiskey (which was sometimes called "gourd corn"). Round *squash* gourds were used as sewing baskets and as containers for the hunter's shot and powder. Polly recalled that her daddy used one to hold the nails in his blacksmith shop. She also remembered that, "We had one that we used for our homemade lye soap—our *soap* gourd.".The little egg-shaped *simling* gourds were used to store garden seeds; were put under the setting hens; were used as darning eggs; and were made into rattles for the baby.

An old square-dance call starts out:

> Sugar in the gourd and powder in the horn
> I never felt so good since I was born.
> Sugar in the gourd and can't get it out
> Take a stick and roll the gourd about.

Apparently the *sugar* gourd even made it to camp meeting, for in another old song the singer recalls that at the camp meeting, "I'd take hold—of the sugar in the gourd—and eat up the Methodist pie." This big sugar-gourd was also used for storing eggs, flour, salt, etc.

A *fat* gourd was used for storing cooking fat, and the earliest pioneers filled gourds with bear oil and a wick to use as lamps. Fred High recalled that the first time he ever struck a sulphur match was when his mother let him strike one to use as a light when he climbed under the floor to get the gourd of copperas that she used in dying cloth. And there is even a community in Jackson County called Gourd Neck.

The *banjo* gourd was made into a simple type of banjo, and a similar type with a long neck is familiar even today as a dipper hanging by the springhouse or the well. Another type with almost no neck and a fat body is also seen today hanging in the trees of country homes as birdhouses or flowerpots. And if those were not enough uses, there was always the *dishrag* gourd. Aunt Alma explains how it got its name: "You can take 'em and peel off that outside, and they make good dishrags—almost like a sponge." All in all it seemed like the gourd was a very handy thing to have around.

WILD PLANTS

Many of the "vittles" for the early settlers' tables came from the woods around them, for the mountain wife excelled in making use of the wild plants that grew in the forest. A family dinner would often include wild greens, such as poke sallet, sorrel, dock, lamb's-quarters, or mustard greens; wild strawberry or blackberry cobbler; black walnuts; root tea; and possum, quail, squirrel, or venison that the husband had killed.

Wild greens were one of the favorite Arkansas dishes. They were usually kept cooking in a soup kettle and were always served with what a Northern boy called "pepper juice." Fred High told the story about the man who went to have dinner with a friend and the friend said, "Well, we don't have much to eat here—only greens and pepper sauce." The man said, "Oh, I never did like greens," to which the friend replied, "Well, help yourself to the pepper sauce."

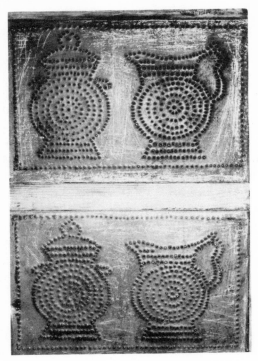

*The pierced tin panels of pie safes were
truly works of art.*

The juice from the greens was often served as a separate
dish known as "pot likker" and was combined with
cornbread to make a full meal. There was a lot of nutrition
in the pot likker and it was an actual dish, not to be
confused with the "por folks'" dishes. These latter
included such things as the skillet tea "made from the
scrapings of the old iron skillet," and the soup that is
described in the story about the man who "said he had a
rabbit head that he had been making soup from. He
loaned it to his neighbor, who lost it—and that stopped the
soup-making for awhile."

In addition to a soup kettle, almost every farm wife had
a pie safe with pierced tin sides. The tin was punched with
the rough side out so the air could circulate but the flies
couldn't get in, which made the designs not only

decorative but useful. Inside, the women kept their cakes and pies made from their treasured old recipes, many of which would be considered uncommon today.

The people in Yell County still recall the extravagant "bud pies" that Mary Wilson made when she picked the buds of the apples that were just forming. Polly said that in the summer they gathered the wild huckleberries, dried them into little hard knots, and used them to make cobblers in the winter. There were buttermilk pies, cornmeal pies, and peanut pies; and here is Mrs. Wilhite's recipe for an old favorite—vinegar pie. (To make your own vinegar see "Aunt Alma's Cure for Sprained Ankles in Horses and Humans" in the section on Folk Remedies.)

VINEGAR PIE

Baked pie shell

Meringue made from three egg whites

3 egg yolks, beaten
1 cup sugar
¼ teaspoon salt

1¾ cup boiling water
¼ cup cider vinegar
¼ cup cornstarch

¼ cup cold water
1 teaspoon lemon
   extract

Place the three egg yolks in the top of a double boiler. Add 1 cup of sugar and ¼ tablespoon salt. Gradually add 1¾ cup boiling water—stirring constantly. Add ¼ cup cider vinegar and ¼ cup cornstarch that has been dissolved in ¼ cup cold water. Cook over boiling water until thick and smooth—about twelve minutes.

Remove from heat. After it cools to lukewarm add 1 tablespoon lemon extract. Stir until smooth and blended good. Scraping the sides of the pan, pour the lukewarm filling into a baked pie shell. Top the pie with frosting (meringue) made from the three egg whites. Brown in the oven.

In addition to food the housewife found other uses for the wild plants around her. John Gideon said, "I remember my grandmother combing her hair with walnut juice to preserve the color." The mullein plants made wicks for lamps, wild herbs were used to cure most illnesses, ground-up acorns were a substitute for coffee, and various plants created dyes for the homespun materials.

After the poke sallet had been eaten in the spring, the same plant went on to produce berries that were used as a purple dye in the fall. In England natural dyes have been used since the earliest times and the expert dyers have passed their recipes for dyeing down through the generations. Various natural dyes that were used in England are still used by mountain dyers. These include walnut shells for dark brown, oak bark for black, blackberry for purple, apple for yellow, and ragweed for orange.

Mrs. Letta Taylor of Wilburn has made an extensive study of natural dyeing and offers the following advice for people who would like to try it:

Dye your clothes with natural materials. It's lots of fun and very exciting. It's easy to do, and you'll be practicing a true art. Some of the natural dye sources are: onion skins, tomato vines, tea, coffee, blackberries, honeysuckle leaves, dandelion and buttercup blossoms, sumac leaves and berries, hickory nuts, and pecan hulls.

These natural dye sources may be found along roadside ditches, in meadows, on hillsides, in lanes, and in backyards—or you might grow them in your garden. Some materials may be found during all the seasons of the year, but the fall colors are more plentiful and will give the richest colors.

As soon as you arrive home put the fruit in a cool place; put leaves, twigs, and bark in water; and spread flower heads and petals out to dry. The sooner you use the materials the richer the dye solution will be.

Mordants are one of the essential things in natural dyeing. Mordant comes from the Latin word meaning to bite and is a substance used to make the color fast. These are some of the mordants that were used in the old days and are still used today: vinegar, alum, copperas, and sodium bicarbonate. (In the very early days they also used rusty nails, iron filings from the blacksmith shop, and chamber water for the setting.) By using different mordants different colors may be obtained with the same plant dyes.

The yarn to be used must be made into skeins for easier handling and to keep it from tangling in the mordanting and dyeing process. I use a chair's legs. Turn the chair upside down. Wind the yarn around two legs into a circle and tie four or five times with cotton cord.

Brew some dyes and see for yourself what striking colors you can get. If you do not grow your own wool, buy natural or white wool—make sure it is 100 percent wool with no additional synthetic fibers. Divide the wool into skeins of about 1/10 of an ounce if you are a beginner. Tie the skeins loosely four or five times with a cotton cord. If the wool is clean and all the oil has been removed, you are now ready to mordant your wool.

Alum is the easiest to use. A good substitute is ammonium alum in a powder form which can be bought at any drugstore or grocery store. It is good on any fiber. Use three ounces of alum to three or four gallons of warm soft water in a large enamel kettle. Stir thoroughly until all has dissolved. Wet one pound of wool skeins in warm soft water and submerge it into the mordant. Simmer for one hour. If vegetable fiber, boil from one hour to two hours.

Let the wool cool in the mordant until it can be handled.

Squeeze out the excess liquid and roll in a towel and put it in the refrigerator until ready to use.

Honeysuckle with alum—color yellow:

Two gallons of cut-up honeysuckle leaves and twigs simmered for two hours in water that they have been soaked in overnight. Remember to keep covered with water. Strain out refuse, return to dye-bath pot. Add wetted half pound mordanted wool to the dye bath. Simmer for thirty minutes, remove from the dye bath, and add two teaspoons of cream of tartar dissolved in a little water to the dye bath and stir; then add the wool to the dye bath and simmer for thirty minutes. Allow to cool in dye bath. Squeeze out of bath, rinse until rinse is clear, and squeeze out water (never twist). Roll up in towels for one to two minutes, then hang up in shade to dry. Remember to shake well to make wool soft and fluffy.

Paper Decorations

We used to make these paper baskets for our "pretties"—we'd hang these at the windows at Christmas.

(Patience)

To decorate their homes people often used a type of folk art known as papyrotamia. This is a fancy name for creations made by cutting designs out of paper. It is an ancient craft that was practiced by the Egyptians as early as 1400 B.C. and is still being used today. Paper cutwork ranges from the elaborate pictures that made up the "traveling exhibits of papyrotamia" in the early 1800's to the simple designs cut by the slaves to decorate their cabins.

Patience learned this art from her grandmother, who was a slave in both Kentucky and Arkansas. When I asked her about it, Patience explained, "We used to cut 'em for the mantlepiece. I thought folks had done quit that. I had

Summer and winter, Patience makes paper decorations to hang on the mantle at Christmas. She wears an amulet on her arm to cure her rheumatism.

done forgot all about that." However, with practiced hands she cut designs out of a long strip of white paper and then cut two hanging baskets out of newspapers.

When the baskets were finished she explained, "You have to put something in there to hold it down. We used to have an apple—we'd put an apple in it." Paper baskets like this were made primarily at Christmas as part of the holiday decorations, but the strips were used to decorate the shelves and the mantle all during the year.

Newspapers were also used as wallpaper, and to repaper the walls was part of any thorough housecleaning. According to a plantation owner, "the people took plain old white biscuit flour and poured boiling water over it to make their paste. Then the newspapers were pasted on the wall, making a useful insulation as well as decoration." This was an old custom noted by Charles Dickens when he visited the United States. In the South he stayed in a log inn that was "tapestried with old newspapers, pasted against the wall."

Aunt Willie claimed she learned to read "sitting around the fire at night reading the newspapers on the wall." She also remembered the time that a new teacher came to teach at the mountain school and put up the first Christmas tree that they had ever seen. The children were reluctant to leave the beautiful tree that day, but they had to hurry home to get ready for the program at school that night. When she got home she found "another unforgettable scene. The floors had been scrubbed white with a shuck mop and the walls papered with clean newspapers my grandfather had brought us. On the table was a cake—surely the finest that was ever baked. And a tired. but happy Mother."

Toys

Store-bought play pretties were few and far between in the early days. But mountain children were as ingenious as

their parents in making toys out of every crumb of waste
material around the farm. One man told me that he was
almost four years old when he spoke his first word. In
recalling the event he said that when he spoke for the first
time he was "playing at the ash hopper, plowing in the
ashes with a goose neckbone." This little boy of eighty
years ago was "plowing" with the one thing he could find
that looked like his daddy's plow.

Various people recalled the playthings that they made
or saw made in the old days. Here are the directions for
some of the simple toys they mentioned:

Bull Roarers (Roy Simpson)—"You take a flat piece of
wood—put a hole through the end—tie a string to it and
you throw it around your head, and it goes to roaring—it
kind of makes a roaring sound . . . This was a very
simple thing that was used by primitive people."

Tom Walkers (Roy Simpson)—"We would use what today
would be called stilts, but we called them Tom Walkers.
We made our own. We just took a couple of strips of wood
and nailed us some pieces on—we just put a piece out here
to keep our foot in. I've even walked footlogs with them
and we would walk through creeks and mud."

Hickory Whistles (Newman Sugg)—"Wait till spring when
the sap comes up, so the bark will slip. Get you a smooth
hickory twig and cut it sloping at one end and square at the
other. Then you cut out a notch just so far down from the
end. Then down here you cut the bark plumb around and
you peck that a little with something to loosen it up, and
you take hold of that bark and just slide it off. And the
bark it's all in one piece—no cracks in it or nothin'. You cut
this notch out here a little bit larger and you trim the wood
and slope that up there for your mouth and put that bark
back on it, and man, that thing'll just blow like a steam
engine. . . . . The smaller the twig the finer the whistle is,
and the bigger the twig the coarser the whistle is."

Compare that description of whistles as they were made

Newman shows how to make hickory whistles.

on Chickalah Mountain with the description given by Kevin Danaher in his chapter "Country Childhood" (from *Irish Country People*). "An old workman showed us how to make sycamore whistles; with a good deal of careful cutting and tapping the bark could be slid off a short length of sycamore twig and then replaced when the twig had been cut to the proper shape, to produce a piercing whistle, very useful for signalling to each other or calling up help in wild games of cops and robbers."

Chewing Gum (Willie Sugg)—"Nobody ever had any kind of bought gum—we got our gum from the sweet gum tree and the pine trees. If you got gum from the sweet gum and put it in a little bucket and boiled it you really had something nice to chew."

Jump Rope (Willie Sugg)—"We played jump the rope with a long thick muscadine vine that we cut in the woods. It took two big girls or boys to throw it. We'd throw 'em 'hot pepper' and if that vine had hit your leg it would have nearly broken it." She said that they ran in the "front door" and in the "back door" and counted to see who was the best jumper—but Aunt Willie, Granny Riddle, and

Bessie Wilhite all said that they did *not* have jump rope rhymes when they were growing up.

Firecrackers—Farmer Wilhite told how the boys "popped cane stalks" to make their firecrackers. When they threw green switch cane—"it had to be green, not dry"—into the fire, every joint in the cane made a loud pop. Fred High told how he had just finished making sorghum one year when, "Some boys came by and popped cane stalks and got the fire out—and burned up two hundred and seventy gallons of good molasses and the shed, and almost burned the pan and mill."

Baseball (Willie Sugg)—"Uncle Newt made his own baseball. He took a long piece of yarn that his mother had spun and he wound it into a tight ball. Then he would kill a squirrel, cut out a piece of the hide, and bury it in wet ashes for three weeks. When the lye from the ashes had eaten all the hair off the hide he washed it off with lye soap and let it dry. The hide was stiff then, but every night while they sat around the fire Newt would work with the hide until it was pliable. Then he cut out strips of the hide to use for lacings and made two patterns out of the hide and laced them over the ball of yarn. That made a fine baseball."

Dolls—The dream of every little girl was to have a china doll. In an old folk song there is a dialogue between a little girl and her mother that starts out:

> Buy me a china doll
>   Do, mama, do, mama;
> Buy me a china doll,
>   Do, mama, do.

The little girl goes on to beg her mother to sell papa's feather bed to get the money for the doll and let papa sleep in the horses' stall, etc. If by any chance a little girl ever did get a china doll, Mother said she didn't play with the doll, but put a ribbon around its waist and hung it on the wall.

Mountain dolls made from: corn cobs, cornhusks, apples, and hickory nuts.

Instead, she probably played with a doll made out of apples, corncobs, flour sacks, cornhusks, buckeyes, dough, hickory nuts, or cotton balls. When the newspapers had been read, pasted on the wall, and cut into designs, the ones that were left were often cut into long strings of paper dolls; when the hollyhocks bloomed, their blossoms made hollyhock dolls; and when the flour was eaten the flour sacks were made into rag dolls.

Myra Adams still makes corncob dolls today and explained that she cuts a corncob into pieces to make the face and then uses a dried bean for the nose, cornsilk for the hair, pipe cleaners for the legs, and makes little baskets out of hickory nuts or acorn caps for them to carry.

String Games—When there was nothing else available there was always a piece of string to tie into a circle and use for string games. Almost all old people remember playing them at school, and playing them with their brothers and sisters as they sat around the fireplace at night. My own children learned them at school and got in the habit of carrying a knotted piece of string around with them to amuse themselves as we traveled. In the summer of 1972 they were doing some of their string tricks in England and other children began comparing old favorites with them and teaching them new ones.

At Oxford we bought a book called *String Games for Beginners* in which the author, Kathleen Haddon, points out that these traditional games often reflect the history and social habits of a people. For this reason they are especially interesting to folklorists, since string games are found all over the world. She points out that "go where you will—to the arctic north or to the coral islands of the Pacific—string games are there." The Eskimo, during their long winters, have made up many games with chants or stories to go with them, and the American Indians as well as the English settlers made string pictures of the things they knew best.

Expedients

There is an old Irish saying, "*Is cuma no muc fear gan seift*"—"The man without an expedient is of no more account than a pig."

(Kevin Danaher)

Here are some typical Arkansas expedients:

Jim Bixler said his nephew was going to get a new watch and Jim told him, "Why don't you do like my great grandad did? He couldn't tell on a cloudy day; but when the sun was shining he had cut notches in the floor and when that sun'd shine in the side of the door he could tell you what time a day it was—and he wouldn't miss it over five minutes either."

When the mule was bad about jumping the fences the pioneers made him a "hobble" or "yoke." They bent a

A hobble being made.

A hobble being worn.

forked green branch around a log and left it until the branch was dry. When the mule had it on he couldn't get through, or over, or under the fence.

Shoe polish was made for protection of the shoes, not just for beauty. Farmer Wilhite told how it was made. "First you get possum grease, bacon grease, chicken fat—any kind of grease. Then you put it on a rag, any kind of old rag will do—it don't have to be your Sunday handkerchief. Next you reach up in the back of the chimney and get some of that black soot and rub it on the rag. You grease your shoes with that and set 'em in front of the fireplace until that grease soaks in and they'll stay waterproof and pliant all winter long."

The best grease of all to go on shoes was polecat grease and a neighbor of the Wilhites, named Tom Cobb, made a business of this. He killed polecats in November, December, and January (the fur-bearing months) to get the fur. Then he rendered the polecat grease and "He had his customers that bought this polecat grease to make their shoe polish from."

MUSICAL INSTRUMENTS

Of a night they'd get together and sing and play music. My grandfather, he was a fiddler. Him and grandma'd get out on the porch of an evening and he'd play the violin and grandma'd beat the neck of it with her knittin' needles. That's the way they passed the time away.

(Jim Bixler)

Arkansas is a land where they make their own music—literally. When Uncle Sam Hess was a little boy he made his first banjo from a gourd—with a squirrel's hide cover and horsehair strings. To make the strings taut he chose long hairs from the horse's mane and tail, wet them, and let them dry on the "banjer." As he did all this he was following an old tradition that had come across the Mississippi with the settlers from the East Coast. In North Carolina, in the 18th century, the people made gourd fiddles with cornstalk bows, and a common name for a banjo was the "gourd shell."

Another mountain banjo player, Floyd Holland, also made his first banjo out of a long-necked gourd, and he still covers his banjo with a piece of deer hide that he tans himself by removing the hair with wet ashes. He describes the first banjo he ever made. "I jest cut the top outta the gourd, you know, and it had a long neck and I put a piece of wood out there fer a fingerboard and let the keys go through the gourd handle. I just made the strings outta sewing thread." Sadly he remembers, "I had to quit playing it though. I kept breaking 'em [the strings], and my mother got after me for using all of her sewin' thread."

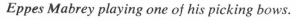

Eppes Mabrey playing one of his picking bows.

Nearby, Bob Blair told how his father used to carve fiddles for the children out of cornstalks, hollowing them out and leaving four strips for strings. Another stalk made the fiddle bow. And if there wasn't time for all that, a stick and a piece of string gave them a pickin' bow.

From these simple beginnings many Ozark musicians have gone on to make some of the loveliest and most unusual musical instruments in the land. Probably the simplest one is the unique mountain picking bow, as turned out by Eppes Mabrey of Mountain View.

This instrument is simply a strip of wood about thirty-eight inches long and three inches wide, curved into an arc, with a string and a key. Eppes makes them out of persimmon wood, white oak, bodark (*bois d'arc*), or cedar. He explains how he does it: "They got to be sawed out with the grain and then you sand them and bore the holes in them for the string. Then you put the keys on them, string them up, and they're ready to play." Today he uses a regular guitar key, but when he first started making them he used a wooden peg like the old-timers had on their fiddles. The key is to tighten and "tune" the bow, and the string is a guitar third string.

Eppes has made three or four thousand of these primitive instruments and sold them to people from all over the country. He says that most people who buy them probably learn to play them, since they are easy to play. One end of the wooden bow is placed against the outside of the jaw and the string is plucked with the thumb or a flat pick. By opening and closing his mouth the player makes various tones and creates the tune. This same type of mouth bow is pictured in the paintings on a cave wall in France dating about 15,000 B.C.

Another old and unusual instrument is the set of quills made and used by Ed Ballentine. These were usually made by the workers out in the canefields, and to make them Ed says, "You just take an old fishing cane, you see, and you just cut 'em. One of 'em's a little coarser'n the other'n.

Ed Ballentine playing the quills.

They got a joint on the end. Cut a gap in the other end. Flatten off a place for your lips."

Playing the quills is sometimes called "hoodling" or "reed-blowing" and is an ancient form of making music. The early settlers brought their quills with them as they moved westward, and the history of Carroll County, Tennessee, mentions that, "In the colony that first landed were fiddlers, banjo-pickers and *reed blowers*."

It was in Tennessee that Ed's father, John Ballentine, learned to play the quills. According to Ed, "He learned it down in Wayne County, Tennessee. A colored boy learned him how to play it." His father, who was born "next year after the Civil War," brought the idea with him when he

Violet Hensley playing a fiddle she made out of buckeye wood.

came to Arkansas in 1880. He came in a wagon train with forty-two wagons, and according to the tales that other people have told about their journeys in a wagon train, there were probably many tunes played with the "quills" around the campfires at night.

This was another custom that was well known in Ireland. Kevin Danaher related in *Irish Country People* how "A stalk of green corn could be made to produce a most fascinating noise; cut off short above a joint and with a slit about an inch long cut downward below the joint it could be put into the mouth and blown like a reed. These we called *deocháns*, and to hear five or six of them with different and discordant notes all being blown together would break the heart of any musician and delight that of any small boy."

More complicated to make than the picking bow or the hoodling stick is the fiddle. One of the best fiddle makers in Arkansas is Mrs. Violet Hensley of Yellville. She learned the technique from her father, and explains how it all came about:

> My daddy was one of a family of fifteen—and his older brother had a fiddle and wouldn't let him play it. So he said, "Somebody made 'em"—he could make his own. So the first one he made, he drove nails in a board and bent his sides between the nails—the shape of a fiddle. Then he kept makin' 'em—he made 'em all by hand—cut his wood with a chopping axe and a crosscut saw. Hand planed it.
>
> When I was fifteen I started out to make my own fiddle. I made my own design by folding a piece of paper and cutting out the shape of a fiddle. The whole fiddle was fourteen inches long and it would play, too. Then I made four by the time I was seventeen. The only help I had outta that—my Daddy had to pull one end of the crosscut saw.

Soon after that she got married and for twenty-seven years she was busy raising her family, not making fiddles. But today she is making them for collectors all over the country. She explains that, "I make the tailpieces out of dogwood, I make the fingerboards out of walnut, and I make the pegs out of persimmon. And I make the tops out of Arkansas pine, spruce, and a new one out of buckeye wood." She uses all hand tools, chops the dogwood down with her chopping axe, and even made her own knife out of a file.

Making your own instruments can lead to some unconventional types of music-makers. Farmer Wilhite took the dimensions of a tenor banjo, the fingerboard of an old guitar, the keys and tailpiece of an old mandolin, and made an unusual type of mandolin.

The instrument has thirty-one ribs making up the body

Farmer Wilhite strumming his mandolin.

Walter and Kermit Moody making a guitar.

of it. He had to boil the ribs in water, and according to his story "cooked the first two batches too hard," but he finally got what he wanted. He made the nut out of bone, and when I asked him what kind, he said "Out of an old piece of steak." This actually makes a large and beautiful instrument which he calls a "bass mandolin." As he rightly says, "I'm entitled to call it anything I want."

Instruments are also made in unusual places. In back of their auto shop the Moody brothers turn out "Jimmy Driftwood" style guitars in their spare time. These instruments are made with spruce tops, maple backs, and mahogany necks. The most distinctive thing about them is their shape, and Kermit explains the reason for this unusual design: "You see how this fits. You know how a guitar's always sliding off. Well, the idea in the shape of this guitar is—it fits. You know, it's not necessary to have it big and thick. You get as much volume out of one like this."

To begin the guitar they shape the top and back, and saw the sides out of ⅛-inch lumber. They glue this together using a homemade press. To make the neck they "saw it out on a bandsaw. Then we shape it, use a wood rasp, you know, the old-time way." The wooden bridge has a bone insert and to make this Kermit says, "We just go to the meat market and get these leg bones of a cow, and boil these anywhere from half a day to a day. And when you take them out—of course they season out—they're just as hard as—you've heard the expression 'as hard as a bone'—well, that's what it is when they dry out. And they're white. You see how white that is. Then I shape it with a sander and cut the little grooves in it for the strings."

The guitars turn out to be interesting and beautiful instruments, and most of all (like all these instrument makers), the Moody brothers are able to say, "We make 'em to our own satisfaction." With folk musicians that seems to be the part that counts the most.

PERSIMMON AND SASSAFRAS TREES

The word "sprouts" does not evoke much emotion in people today, but it sent shivers down the spine of the early Arkansas farmer. For, once the fields were cleared of rocks and the crops were planted, the settler was faced with the problem of persimmon and sassafras sprouts that constantly threatened to overtake his land. Some farmers kept goats in their fields to eat out the sprouts (just as some cotton farmers kept geese to eat out the weeds), but for most farmers these pesty plants had to be cut down by hand throughout the summer.

The disgust they caused the farmer is illustrated in this story related by Fred High. "A man had some sprouts to cut and he said, 'I will take off four days next week and cut them sprouts.' So the next week he went out and looked them over and said, 'Oh, I can cut them in three days,' and went back to the house. Next day he went out and taken a good look and said, 'Oh, I can cut them in two days' and went back to the house again. Then on the fourth day he taken his hoe in dead earnest and flew into them like a man fighting a bull. He did this for a while—then he taken another good look and said, 'Any fool would know that I couldn't cut these in one day,' so he threw down his hoe and went back to the house again.'"

Since these sprouts became trees almost overnight, it didn't take the Ozark farmer long to learn how to "make do" with the ones that were growing outside of the fields. The persimmon tree provided a fruit that is often called the "Ozark date." It is smaller than the California or Oriental persimmon but is full of vitamins A and C and was used to make persimmon cake, puddings, cookies, and even persimmon beer. The important thing was to make sure that the fruit was fully ripe since it made the mouth "drawy" if it was picked before the first frost. Once the fruit was picked it was pushed through a sieve to make a pulp and used in many recipes, like—

MRS. BELL'S PERSIMMON COOKIES

Mix 1 cup sugar, 1 egg, ½ cup shortening, 1 cup persimmon pulp, 1 teaspoon soda, ¼ teaspoon cloves, ½ teaspoon nutmeg, ½ teaspoon cinnamon, 2 scant cups flour, 1 teaspoon salt, ½ cup nuts, and ½ cup raisins.
Drop on cookie sheet and bake ten minutes at 350°.

The persimmons that weren't used for cooking right away could be stored in either of two ways. Clean, whole persimmons were packed with alternating layers of brown sugar in airtight crocks. Another method of preservation was to roll the pulp out on the table and dry it into a piece of "persimmon leather." This could be cut into squares and used like dates or raisins.

Any leftover persimmons were used to feed the hogs to make their meat sweeter. The leaves from the tree were dried to make green persimmon tea; the sap from the tree was used for drops to cure earaches; the branches were the preferred stick for many water witchers; and persimmon was one of the favorite woods for making gluts (wooden wedges) for splitting rails.

Like the persimmon tree, every inch of the sassafras tree was used by the thrifty pioneer. Beginning at the top, the small leaves were gathered in the spring, washed, and laid out to dry. When they were completely dry they were crumbled up fine, made into the spice that we know as filé powder, and used to season foods throughout the year. Because of their delicious and unusual smell, the limbs and trunks of the tree were used in a number of special ways:

> They were mixed in with the hickory limbs to burn in the smokehouse and flavor the meat. (But according to an old superstition they were never burned in the cabin, where it was said that sassafras burning in the fireplace would burn up next year's crop.)
>
> They were used to make the roosts in the henhouse because it was believed that the sassafras odor kept the chicken mites away.
>
> The limbs were used to stir the lye soap to give it a good smell. One old recipe for lye soap even called for the addition of "5c worth of sassafras extract."
>
> Sometimes the trunk was cut, holes were bored in it, and the holes were stuffed with homegrown tobacco leaves. As the tobacco dried out it absorbed some of the tree's sap, and when the "plug tobacco" was removed it had a subtle sassafras flavor.
>
> Often the trunk was used for a trough to salt down the hogs at slaughtering time in order to give them a good smell and taste. In describing an early Arkansas hog-killing, Gerstaeker mentioned that "a young man cut a large sassafras tree and out of it he carved half a dozen wooden vessels, five of them to be used for the meat and the other for the lard."

The bark of the tree was stripped and used in several ways: it was used to make a reddish-brown dye; it was mixed with the roots to make the basis for sassafras jelly and that favorite springtime blood-thinner, sassafras tea; and a handful of bark was mixed in with the dried fruit that was stored in the fruit cellars so that the sassafras odor would keep the fruitbugs away. When a coon or possum was baked in the oven they were often laid on a bed of sassafras sticks to give them flavor. Some people used sassafras twigs for their snuff brushes (although one man said that in his family they preferred that part of the blackgum where "the twig joined the branch" because the blackgum was tough and bland). Today people still dip snuff, but very few dip a twig in the snuff and walk around with the "snuff stick" protruding from their mouths.

Sassafras oil was used for insect bites, and sassafras may even have been used for bread, since there is an old community called "Sassafras Pone" in Washington County.

If your field is overrun with sprouts you might like this recipe for Persimmon Bread with Sassafras Icing. It makes use of both kinds of sprouts!

3½ cups flour	4 eggs, beaten
2 teaspoons soda	⅔ cup water
1½ teaspoons salt	1 cup salad oil
2 teaspoons cinnamon	2 cups persimmon pulp
2 teaspoons nutmeg	1 cup raisins
3 cups sugar	1 cup chopped pecans

Sift together the flour, soda, salt, cinnamon, and nutmeg. Stir in the sugar. Add eggs, water, oil, and persimmon pulp. Stir until blended and add raisins and nuts. Pour mixture into greased loaf pans and bake for one hour at 350°. Make a thin white icing, using strong sassafras tea as the liquid. Dribble over the top and sides of the bread.

Today there are very few people who make use of the
persimmon and sassafras trees in all these old ways. But
the trees' autumn foliage, bright gold for the persimmon
and dark red for the sassafras, is a constant joy to modern
travelers, just as it must have been to the early pioneers.

Postscript—Some Thoughts on Making do

The self-sufficiency and ingenuity of the pioneers who
made do with whatever they had at hand was truly
amazing. But this same trait has led to some grim results in
this modern day. The early settler could think of a dozen
uses for the lowly gourd plant, which fortunately had
beautiful vines that wound around his cabin. Unfortunately, his great-grandson surrounds his home with worn-out
refrigerators, broken-down cars, and general junk, thinking that some day he may find a use for, or have a need
for, all this stuff.

It is hard for a tourist passing by and seeing a beautiful
old split rail fence "decorated" with the hubcaps of a dozen
wrecked cars to appreciate the make-do trait that runs
through most mountaineers. I hope this book will help a
little, for even when we can't enjoy these eyesores we can
at least comprehend the idea behind them.

Another thought about making do concerns the
"authentic pioneer crafts" seen at some of the arts fairs.
Many of the objects listed in this section were things that
we would call "crafts," such as pine-needle baskets and
corncob dolls; but crafts as such were almost nonexistent
in pioneer days. The early settler rarely ever made
anything that he didn't intend to use. As Roy Simpson
explained, "Folk art was scarce on hill farms, but folk
objects existed in large numbers . . . . They made no
paintings, ceramics, or glassware, though there were
quilts, knitted articles, and sometimes whittled-out ob-

jects." (Of course there were exceptions. He told about the time one man painted a picture of a mule and wrote underneath it: "This is a mule." As Mr. Simpson said, "Everybody seemed to think it was a good thing he wrote what it was under it!")

If you are looking for authentic folk articles remember that all crafts are not necessarily traditional folk art. Pioneers were soap-makers but not glass blowers, they made containers out of gourds but not out of plastic bleach bottles; they made dolls out of apples but not out of Coke bottles with styrofoam heads; they made candles out of beeswax or animal fat, but they did not make multicolored candles in the shape of tulips or owls; and it is safe to say that no pioneer homestead had an ashtray made out of an elongated pop bottle, or a wastebasket made out of egg cartons. (Their fireplace served both purposes nicely.)

Even whittling is a social art more than a craft.

CHAPTER 7
FOLKLORE

This section is a collection of the oral heritage of the people of Arkansas—place names and their origins, folk sayings of various communities, hunting stories, etc. The term folk*lore* is used to distinguish it from the earlier part of the book which dealt primarily with the material aspects of Arkansas folk life.

This part also contains a group of lore that I have called "superstitions and beliefs." There is a fine line, sometimes too fine to be seen, between superstition and fact. Very often an old superstition or a folk cure will turn out to be scientifically accurate, or at least to have a logical explanation. Therefore I have lumped superstitions, weather and moon lore, folk beliefs, and cures all in one lot; and I will let the reader draw the line for himself.

PLACE NAMES

The name of Arkansas itself is wrapped in folklore. Some say it was used by the upstream Indians who referred to the Indians living along the lower Mississippi and Arkansas rivers as the Akansa or Arkansas, meaning the "downstream people." Others say that a tribe of

Indians who separated from the Kansas Nation were famous for the quality of their bows or "arcs." Because of this they were called the Arc-Kansas, and eventually the Arkansas. Whatever its origin, the name became the title for the territory and then the state, and was finally the subject of a wild speech supposedly given before the state legislature and entitled, "Change the Name of Arkansas, Hell No."

One of the most fascinating things about Arkansas (or any state) is the way some of the creeks, towns, and mountains got their names. In the early days almost every town was built beside a creek, and there are dozens of these streams with the name of Crooked Creek, Lick Creek, Mill Creek, and even Dishwater Creek. The origin of these names is obvious; but it is harder to explain where Dancing Rabbit, Huzzah, Horsehead, Butcherknife, Sugar Orchard, and Hog Tusk creeks got their names.

Sometimes you can find an old settler who knows the origin. Uncle Aaron Stevens told how Roastin' Ear Creek got its name: "Way back years ago they had this creek all in corn, you know, and it come a big rise [flood] and it washed in some of the fields—and washed the corn out. And the corn come floatin' down the creek, and they called it Roastin' Ear Creek."

Hog Scald Creek was named for the kettlelike holes in it. The pioneers used to drop red-hot rocks in them to heat the water and scald their hogs there at hog-killing time. These same holes, cleansed by the ever-flowing stream, were used at camp-meeting time for baptisms.

Occasionally a name came about as the corruption of another name. One of my favorite water witchers lives in the Ouachita Mountains in a place called Mars Creek, named for the Mars (Meyers) family, who first settled there. And a friend of mine told me about one of her good friends who was through with college and living out of the state when one day she was looking at a map of Arkansas and realized with horror that the place that she and

How did this beautiful place get the terrible name of Hag's Holler? (Yell County.)

everyone else in her hometown had always called the Nars, was really spelled the Narrows. Low Freight Creek came from L'eau Frais Creek and the Fush River is actually the Fourche la Favre.

The rocks in the field around this old cabin show how Stone County got its name.

People of the Ozarks are often very literal when it comes to naming things. Just as they call the little flies that buzz around their homemade wine "drunkards," and the short cotton of the mountains "shoetop cotton," so there are at least two counties where a small series of hills is called the "Tater Hills." Roy Simpson said Slick Rock Gap got its name because, "They had a slick rock over there—the water came out over it and the moss grew on it." The strip of red clay running from Marcella to St.

James gave the community of Red Stripe its name. (Later the people gave it the more appealing name of Pleasant Grove, just as the people of Frog Level changed their town to Magnolia.)

Mrs. Essie Ward was raised on Nubbin Mountain, which is smaller than its neighbors, just as a nubbin is smaller than the other ears of corn. (Having to perform a trivial task is sometimes referred to with disgust as "shuckin' a nubbin'.") Boat Mountain is shaped like a boat and Sugar Loaf Mountain is rounded on top like the loaves of brown sugar that the pioneers used. Birdseye supposedly got its name from the Indians who said it was a tiny spot, no bigger than a "bird's eye." The community of Bucksnort was said to have received its name when an old man came home drunk one night and his wife yelled out (for all the town to hear) that he was just an old fool out buckin' and snortin' around. (Another explanation for the name of Bucksnort was that it was "so called because it was a rendezvous for deer in the early days.") When I asked some men sitting in front of the general store, playing dominoes, how the town of "Loafer's Glory" got its name, they said, "Lady, you're looking at it!"

A church in the community of Bluffton has always gone by the name Scrouge Out (to be "scrouged" is to be crowded) and is even referred to that way in the newspaper: "There will be a homecoming at the Pleasant Hill Church, better known as Scrouge Out." (Article in the *Yell Country Record*.) Irene Williams, who grew up there, said, "They told me that in the early days so many people came to church that they couldn't get inside the house and they got to calling it Scrouge Out." Another woman told Roy Simpson how the community of Little Hope got its name. When they built the school there someone said, "What shall we call it?" and the woman's father said, "We'll call it Little Hope, for we have little hopes of it ever amounting to anything."

Aunt Chat told how her father named two places. "When they was threshin' wheat—everywhere they'd thresh wheat they'd eat their dinner. And they'd always have turnip greens and hog jowl cooked for dinner. And they eat it too. And Pa called it [the community] Hog Jowl. And everything Pa put a name on, well, it just wore . . . . They's a bunch of little hills between here [Pine Ridge] and Mena—there's seven of 'em. *Now* then they're graded down till you can just drive right on. But in those days when we'd get to them it was a dead pull—over the top, and over the top, and over the top. The teams was give out; the wagons would get bogged down. So Pa named them the Seven Devils, and they still go by that."

The most confusing terms to an outsider in an area will be the unusual ways that place names are pronounced. Often an *a*, *ea*, or *ia* on the end of a word becomes a *y*, so that Mt. Ida, Mt. Judea, and Onia are pronounced Mt. Idy, Mt. Judy, and Ony. Chickalah (Sha-kee'-lah) Mountain, where Newman and Lillie live, has the same pronunciation as the old Indian orator that it was named for.

Even common words are sometimes pronounced differently. A friend of ours who lives in the Ozarks was telling me how some of the local mountains got their names. One was called Cow Mountain. He said that in the days when buffalo roamed the area all the animals in one herd had been killed except one old cow that always eluded the hunters. They never did catch her, and after she died a natural death the people named the mountain in her honor. Then he explained that the next mountain was called Painter Mountain because the largest painter ever killed in those hills was shot on that mountain. I thought it was one thing to kill buffalo, but it was another thing to kill painters, no matter how bad their art. However it turned out that the people were simply using an old mountain pronunciation, not for an artist, but for a panther (pān'ter).

REMEDIES

In England nearly every village had a "wise woman" who knew the secrets of the wild herbs that grew in the hedgerows. In the Ozarks their descendants became "granny-women," who knew the secrets of the wild plants growing in the forests. Here are some of the cures that have been passed down through the generations to their descendants.

For snakebite many people believed in the healing qualities of a wild plant called the snakeweed. Aunt Alma said that her grandmother was a midwife who gathered wild herbs to make her own medicine. One day the grandmother and her daughter, "Aunt Emma," were out in the woods gathering herbs, when they found proof of the benefit of the snakeweed. As Aunt Alma told it:

> They went out to get their herbs to fix their medicine and things, and this rattlesnake and king snake was fighting. So they went to watching. And this king snake would get so sick that it would just straighten out. And it would go to this one weed and eat it. And then it'd come back and it'd fight that rattlesnake again. And it did that several times. And finally it killed that rattlesnake. And when they got through fighting Grandmother and Aunt Emma went to see and it was a snakeweed, was what that king snake went and eat. And it killed that big rattlesnake—it was a huge thing!

Uncle Aaron Stevens gave his own snakebite cure —"Kill him [the snake] right there and just cut a piece out of him and put the flesh side down right next to the bite and it'll draw the poison right out. My wife got snake bit and that's what they done for her."

Aunt Willie told about the time Uncle Loyd was bitten on the heel by a snake and came home screaming. Grandmother hurried to kill a chicken and put the flesh against the bite (an old remedy from her home state of

Georgia). Grandpa came running with the bottle of whiskey. And when they sent for the doctor, he sent back word to mix salt and egg yolk together and put on it. That took care of everybody's favorite remedy, and one of them must have worked, since the only bad effect that Uncle Loyd had was that every year at that very same time of year the spot on his heel would break out in a rash.

Another day Aunt Willie told about the time a boy at their little country school was bitten by a rattlesnake. The teacher asked if anybody knew for sure they had sound teeth, and of course nobody knew because they had never been to a dentist. "So the teacher said, 'Well, I know I do have.' He washed off the boy's foot and got down and sucked all the poison out and the boy didn't even get sick."

For jaundice, hepatitis, etc., Newman gave an old remedy used by his great-grandfather. "My great-grandpa, Sims Suggs, he would use honey, and then he'd take a deer's horn, and he'd burn that horn until it was just a pile of ashes. Then he'd mix this honey with those ashes from that deer's horn. And then he'd give it—I don't know exactly what the regular dosage each day was, but the honey was the main ingredient. I don't know what would be in a deer's horn of any medical value." This was apparently based on an old English remedy. At Oxford University one of the relics of New College is a unicorn horn presented to the college in 1458. The tip of the horn is missing, since it was cut off for the Earl of Leicester during Queen Elizabeth's reign. The Earl had sent for the entire horn to grind into powder and use as an antidote for poison, but instead he received only the tip of the horn.

Aunt Alma gave her cure for sprained ankles in horses and humans. Her first advice was to always have ready a jar of homemade cider vinegar. To make this you save all the parings from your apples and put them in a big jar with some water and sweetenin'—either honey or sorghum. When this turns to vinegar it is ready to use. To cure a sprain you mix the vinegar with red clay into a thick paste, put it on the sore spot, and bind it with rags. She claimed that she used this method to cure one of Uncle Ed's horses that had a sprained ankle, used it on her own sprained ankles, and even used it on one of the horses that was at Hot Springs for the annual racing meet.

Annie Campbell had a slightly different (and easier) cure for sprains: "Heat some vinegar and saturate a cloth in this hot vinegar and wrap it around the affected part. Then sleep with your foot in a brown paper sack."

Apparently the pioneers believed that the worse the smell the more potent the medicine. John Gideon said a favorite poultice was a "tobacco juice and onion pack." He also remembered that their medicine "consisted of skunk oil, coal oil, and turpentine"; and he described another common remedy: "Asafetida was put in a tobacco sack and tied to a string. This was worn around the neck to ward off croup, colds, and most diseases." Roy Simpson agreed:

> Many hill folk thought the wearing of a sack of asafetida suspended against the chest by a string about the neck was a protection against colds. I am inclined to believe there may be something in it, for even a cold germ might well back down when faced with the odor of asafetida.

Newman told how they packed sugar around open sores and bandaged them to cure infection. He said they frequently used laudanum and opium—in fact, his mother kept a bottle of laudanum hidden in a little side panel of the old clock, and "They banked on that laudanum." Uncle Aaron told how they had a madstone for rabies that his uncle had taken out of a white deer.

Aunt Chat said her mother was a marvelous doctor. She gave some of her mother's favorite remedies:

> When we got malarial and took the chills they'd gather dogwood berries and take nine berries—three a day, one at a time, till you take nine. And then you waited three days,

and you took three more today, three more another day, and three more another day. Now that was to cure the chills. Or boil this old dead sagebrush and make tea and drink that. Wow! If we coulda just got one bottle of Raleigh's Chill Tonic that woulda knocked the whole thing. But that wasn't a-goin' then.

And then she made a worm medicine that really got the job done. She mixed up a little castor oil, twenty grains of calomel, and fifteen drops of wormseed oil. She gave a teaspoon of that—oh, just owings to the age you know—if they began to get sick on it she'd quit it. But that really got the worms gone.

We had everything that was to give away like that. [Chicken pox, measles, etc.] We had smallpox—there was twenty-two of us at our house. Pa, he just went out and gathered them in, and he'd gather in another family. He let 'em stay in bed three days with the fever and when that three days' fever was over, he'd say, 'Come on, let's go to work.' He didn't care whether we'd go to work or not, but it'd get us out in the air. A friend of ours at Mena—they took him to the Pest House before Pa could get him. That's where they took the smallpox people—put 'em all in a room and there they stayed.

Aunt Willie said Grandmother made various medicines by mixing wild cherry bark with whiskey, sulphur with molasses, rock candy with whiskey, and quinine with an egg white (so it would "slip down"). Quinine was often used to cure the chills, and since it was so bitter it was usually mixed with peaches; so that quinine and peaches was a common spring tonic.

Another type of old remedy is known as the "transference of evil," and supposedly comes from the customs of early, barbarous peoples. A relic of this is found in the belief of people who try to remove a sty from their eye by standing in the center of a crossroad and reciting the verse:

Sty, sty, leave my eye,
And get on the next person who passes by.

They got rid of their warts by transferring them to the hogs. "Cut a potato and rub the cut side on the warts and feed the potato to the pigs—they'll get your warts."

The value of bees in curing arthritis was well known, and Jim Bixler told of his experience:

> I had arthritis so bad—back in about 1950. I got so bad that I couldn't bird hunt—and you know I had to be pretty bad then. My right leg—I had to drag it around when I walked.
>
> A friend told me to start handling bees if I wanted to get cured. The stings do it. You don't *let* 'em sting you—you'll naturally get stings ever time, you know. They'll get up your pants leg and you'll mash 'em—you can't blame 'em for stinging you if you mash 'em.
>
> I never had any arthritis since then and I had really had it bad.

If all these remedies failed, an Arkansan could always pack his family in the wagon and head for one of the many medicinal springs. A glance at the map shows that he had a choice of at least twenty-five towns with springs in their name. In the early days people believed in their healing powers and traveled many miles to reach them.

There were sixty-three springs at Eureka Springs and they were visited by the Indians and pioneers alike. A woman whose mother lived there in the early 1880's wrote me a description of the town as it was in those days: "Tents was over hillside with people in them. With all kind sickness. They thought the water cure any thing."

People also camped in tents at Heber Springs, where the curative effects of the water were more selective. There were seven springs and each had its own specialty—the eye spring cured sore eyes, the stomach spring cured ulcers, the black sulphur, red sulphur, and white sulphur springs got their names because "you put a coin in there, a silver coin, and it turns it those colors," the iron spring cured anemia, the magnesium spring cured whatever was left.

As neighbors discuss the weather and swap tall tales, folklore lives on. Maybe one reason Arkansas has such a rich folk heritage is given by Roy Simpson. He explained that in the hills, "neighbor" is a verb, and the worst thing one hillman can say about another is: "He won't neighbor with me.".

SAYINGS

Wherever you go in Arkansas you are never far from the country. Both yesterday and today this has been a land of farms, and even city folks use expressions related to farm life. When someone has a hard job to do, people often say: "He has a long row to hoe"; when all the children are grown and gone they say: "The chicks have flown the coop"; and a businessman who hasn't been hungry lately will say: "I'm off my feed" (like a cow) or remark about a competitor that "He has to root hog or die." When he gets sleepy he says he is going to bed with the chickens; it's time to go home when "the sun's gettin' up into the shank of the evenin'"; and if his coffee isn't strong enough he claims it is "weaker'n well water." About someone who is lazy he'll say, "He's a good ole dog but he don't like to hunt." These and other folk sayings indicate the rural origins of the state.

In various communities there are many expressions that are strictly local in origin, but have been handed down from generation to generation until they have become a part of the language. The following is a collection of some of these old sayings, with (whenever possible) an explanation of the origins of each phrase. Most of them give evidence that the pioneers were close observers. Their mother wit enabled them to laugh at each other and themselves—and to make a hard life bearable.

The originator of one settlement's most popular expression was Uncle Jim Hatch, whose wife, Cindy, was known throughout the community for her contrariness. Whatever was proposed—Cindy opposed it. The Hatches lived on one side of a wide creek and the meetinghouse was on the other side, so that in order to get to church they had to walk a footlog across the water. One Sunday morning as they were crossing on the slippery log, Cindy fell in. Afterward, when friends asked why the Hatches missed church that morning, Uncle Jim told how they were crossing the creek when he heard a loud "kersplash," and turned to see what had happened. And he shook his head in resignation as he told his friends sadly, "Thar lay Cindy—headin' upstream!"

Another time a man in this same little town complained to his neighbor, who was a very slow-witted old man, that the moles were ruining his garden. The old man said that he could cure this by getting a sack and holding it over the holes so that the moles would crawl up in it. The man agreed to let the old man try this remedy, even though he knew it was impossible; and told him that he would give him a dollar if he caught four moles by sundown the next day. Early the next morning the dim-witted old man was sitting in the garden holding his brown paper bag over one of the mole holes; and soon word spread all over town that he was trying to catch four moles in a sack. Late that afternoon, just before sundown, a crowd gathered, and someone asked him how he was doing. He called out cheerfully, "Pretty good, pretty good. This 'un I'm atter and three more, and I'll have four."

On another day a woman looked out her upstairs window into her next door neighbor's backyard and was horrified to see that the neighbor's children were out back having a fight with some freshly churned butter. Feeling certain that her neighbor would want to know that her children were ruining all the butter as well as getting it all over themselves, she rushed over to tell her. After listening to the woman's story the neighbor calmly replied in her most disdainful voice, "Well, them's *my* kids and *my* butter."

Despite the hard life the mountain settlers led, they often pampered their children. There was a mother whose little girl whined and complained from daylight to dark. Sometimes when the mother could stand it no more and said so, the little girl would hang her head to one side and sadly say, "Ma, why don't you git me a cookie and see if that'll git me to hesh."

In this same area lived the Apples, who were terrible question-askers. One day Uncle Sid was driving his team down the road when he passed one of the Apple boys. They stopped to talk and pretty soon the Apple boy asked, "Sid, what's your horses' names?" Uncle Sid said, "Pete and Tobe." The Apple boy asked, "Which un's Pete?" Uncle Sid pointed him out. The Apple boy stood there a long time and finally he asked, "Which un's Tobe?"

And nearby, on Chickalah Mountain, there was an old man who lived alone and didn't have anybody to cook for him. He was such an awful bore that no one ever wanted to invite him home with them. Every Sunday after church he would go up to my great-grandpa (or someone else in the congregation) and say, "Alfred, you know how you're always atter me to come home with you. Well, today I think I'll come."

All the incidents above occurred in the communities where my grandparents were raised. These expressions have been used, not only in our family, but throughout those communities for many generations. When we want to express someone's obstinancy we say, "Thar lay Cindy—headin' upstream"; and if we say, "Give her a cookie and see if that'll git her to hesh," you know that someone's complaining is driving us crazy. On the other hand we will tell you "This un I'm atter and three more and I'll have four" to express optimism in the face of insurmountable odds. Likewise we may invite ourselves over to each other's house with, "You know how you're always atter me to come home with you?" or indicate a stupid question with, "Which un's Tobe?" But when we say "Them's *my* kids and *my* butter"—beware! That's mountain talk for mind your own business.

To indicate that someone is more sophisticated than the rest, we'll say, "He's been places and et in ho' tels"—a saying that harks back to the days when only a few people traveled to places where they had no family to stay with. And many meals in our family have ended with this exchange that supposedly took place between a deaf old man and his son-in-law many, many years ago:

> Son-in-law (at the end of a big meal): Well, I've et sufficient.
> Old man: Said ya went a-fishin'?
> Son-in-law: Said I had aplenty.
> Old man: Said ya caught twenty?
> Son-in-law (in disgust): Oh, you old fool!
> Old man (sympathetically): Aw, you broke your pole.

Sometimes an expression is no good without the gestures that go with it. Once Uncle James Rutledge told someone how "That red muley horned Melvin down the other day." This was repeated all over the community for years and made everyone laugh for two reasons. First, whoever told it would twitch their nose sideways the way

Uncle James always did when talking. Also, a muley is a cow that doesn't *have* any horns.*

Here are some other family expressions that people have told me about: My neighbor said that her grandmother always declared, "It'll never be noticed on a gallopin' horse" when she wanted to urge them not to pay too much attention to little details. This same grandmother believed that only absolutely necessary work should be done on the Sabbath, so anything done on Sunday was called "gettin' the ox outta the ditch." (Other people use this expression to indicate impossible tasks.) Another friend told me that her mother-in-law always said, "We've got goose eggs and new overalls" to indicate "We're doing all right."

The expression "hot enough to fry spit" came from her mother's habit of spitting on the iron to see if it was the right temperature, according to one woman. Faye Underwood explained the expression "coon a log." "You see, years ago there were no bridges and when going to the store, church, or whatever, you had to find a tree that was down across the creek. Sometimes you were able to walk

---

*The muley seems to have an important place in comical folklore. An old song, supposedly one of George Washington's favorites, has a verse that goes:

Grandpa had a muley cow, 'us muley when it 'us born,
It took a jaybird forty years to fly from horn to horn.

("The Darby Ram")

In another old song, a young girl sends her lover a list of impossible tasks, including this:

Go tell him to clear me one acre of land
....
Go tell him to plow it with a muley-cow's horn,
And plant it all over with one grain of corn.

("Rose, Marrow, and Thyme")

And an Arkansas ballad relates that:

When they go to farm, I'll tell you what they plow
A little muley calf or a long horn cow
And here they go with a whoop-gee-haw,
And that's about the way of Arkansas.

("The Arkansas Boys")

Another way to say "Mind your own business." This sign on a store in the Ouachitas is reminiscent of the sign Otto Ernest Rayburn claimed to have seen in the Ozarks: "NOTIS! trespassers will B persecuted to the full extent of 2 mungrel dogs which never was over-sochible to strangers & 1 dubble brl. shot gun which ain't loaded with sofa pillors."

these as footlogs, but if the water was high and all, little ones had to sit down, straddle that log, and kind of frog hop across the creek on that log. That was called coonin' a log."

As they told stories about various aspects of folklore, many of the people mentioned in this book used colorful or unusual expressions that were more descriptive than standard English could ever be. Here are some of the phrases that don't appear elsewhere in the book:

When Farmer Wilhite was telling about the time the revenuers came to Greasy Cove to capture the moonshiners, he said, "They cleaned that place out. And they didn't leave enough men and boys to split kindlin'!" In describing a snake he said it could "open its mouth big enough to swallow a goose egg, pert near." Fred High, when discussing a public appearance he was to make, warned, "I will be as awkward as a cow gigging fish." Another time he wrote that, "A man in a lawsuit without money is like a one-legged man at a kicking." One man told how people started calling him by a certain nickname and they used it so often that it "stuck like a cow in a bog."

When you ask people how they're doing, you are liable to get some unusual answers. Caroline Rainbolt, talking about having the flu, declared that she was "so sick I'd a had to got better to of died." Mr. F. Q. Browne, of Sheridan, said people declared they were "grunting" to mean they weren't feeling healthy: and Mother said a common response to "How are you?" was "Well, we've been a-chillin' lately" (had malaria). When Uncle Aaron Stevens wanted to say that a calf was sick, he said that it "had ever hair turned the wrong way."

To indicate how they're doing financially, people will say, "We're too poor to paint and too proud to whitewash," or "We're living off the back forty" (meaning, "We're barely getting by"). Others will say, "We're living high on the hog" (meaning, "We're eating hams—doing well"). And to describe how well-off he was as a child, Roy Simpson said: "I had enough overalls and shirts so that I did not have to go to bed while my mother washed for me."

He went on to tell why he didn't very often dance: "My father had a saying, ''bout as graceful as a bird they call the bear,' and I was about that graceful." Farmer Wilhite remembered that as kids they always thought this old saying was funny: "I come to borrow the scissors. We're gonna have a cuttin' and a slashin' over at our house tonight. Mammy's gonna cut up a blanket and make Dad a new pair a britches, and then she's gonna cut up Dad's old britches and make me a new pair a britches."

Mr. Browne said they used the expression "light a shuck" to mean hurry because "In olden days matches were scarce and twisted cornshucks were used to carry fire from one place to another—and shucks burn fast." He also noted that "two whoops and a holler" always meant a short distance. Often one person will say another is not very "high larnt" to indicate that the other person is uneducated.

When Aunt Chat was talking about hard work, she said,

"Don't tell me we didn't scratch" (like the chickens); and in discussing her husband's good temper, she said he "never did have an outburst of madness." One day, as we walked up on the Tallent's porch right at noon, Polly called out, "Are we hindering your dinner, Brother Lonzo?" Aunt Willie once scoffed about a "careful" woman, "She was so stingy she wouldn't put an egg in her cornbread"; and like many other teachers she recalled about someone, "He went his first school to me."

Certain words have an uncommon meaning for rural people. For example, when they say "country" they mean a much smaller area than most people realize. Floyd Holland said, "I've witched for wells all over the country—all out on the mountain, and some in Van Buren County." And Aunt Chat recalled, "That was over in another country, that was six miles up the way." Again, she was telling about an event that happened "over in another country," which couldn't have been too far away because she went on to say, "I could hear the dogs bark from here." Ed Ballentine said about his father, "He was fourteen when he come to this country." By country he meant not the United States, but Arkansas.

In addition to all of these general expressions there are certain specialized terms that various groups use. We have seen how bee hunters and sorghum-makers had their own vocabulary. Children were another group who had a language all their own. For example, boys playing marbles used certain expressions that might sound foreign to an outsider. According to Mother:

> In the marble game the person who got to make the rules was the one who was lucky. You decided by chance who would have the first turn, and that person could make the rules. If he didn't say "venture rounduns"—you can't "move around" is what it meant, but "rounduns" is what they called it—then you could move to a better place. If he didn't say "venture fudge," then he couldn't penalize you for moving your taw up a little closer to the ring. You had

one special one that was your "taw" that you used to shoot the others. If he didn't call out the rules then you could fudge up a little and get closer to the ring or you could move around for a better position.

These were old expressions and were similar to ones related by William Newell in his book on children's games. He says:

Extensive is the lore of marbles. When a lad wishes to change his position, so that, while preserving the same distance from his mark, he may have a more favorable position, he exlaims, "Roundings." If, however, his antagonist is quick enough, he will cry "Fen (defend) roundings." The game, when played to win the marbles of the opponent, is said to be "in earnest."

Another group who had their own language were the railroad workers. Lillian Hale gave me this list of terms that her husband, Joe Hale, used when he worked for the railroad. These were names that the railroad men had for each other: a track worker was a "gandy dancer"; a yard clerk was a "mud hop"; a billing clerk was a "bill buster"; a locomotive engineer was a "hog head"; a switchman was a "snake"; a brakeman was a "brakie"; and a car repairman was a "car knocker."

One of the most interesting folk terms is the expression "suggins," used to indicate "por folks." This has led to the formation of a Suggin Society to study the humble parts of Arkansas' past, and has also led to a lot of discussion as to the origin of the word. Since it is a folk word it is hard to know exactly where it came from, but these things we do know: it is pronounced soo-gin; it was originally meant as an insult ("Don't act like a suggin" was often said to children); and it is used primarily by people living along the White River.

Another derogatory term in the river country is "peckerwood," which is sometimes Negro slang for "poor

Peckerwood sawmill in the Ozarks. "You'd take logs to the sawmills and they'd saw 'em on the halves. The sawmill man he got half the lumber and you got half." (Warren Wilhite.)

whites." In the mountains "peckerwood" is used both as a substitute for "woodpecker" and also in scorn. It could be with either meaning in mind that two of the verses of "Skip to My Lou" say:

> Pretty as a redbird, prettier too,
> Pretty as a redbird, prettier too,
> Pretty as a redbird, prettier too,
> > Skip to My Lou, My Darling.

> If you can't get a redbird, a peckerwood'll do,
> If you can't get a redbird, a peckerwood'll do,
> If you can't get a redbird, a peckerwood'll do,
> > Skip to My Lou, My Darling.

Many people expect to hear the mountaineer say "you-all" to indicate more than one person, but a much more common expression is "you'uns." When a guest gets ready to leave, a good host says "You'uns needn't run off." Often rural people will use words that sound out of place, such as "either" with a long *i*, and "dreamt," as when Aunt Chat said, "He dreamt that this ladder was raised from earth to heaven."

In his book, *Down in the Holler, A Gallery of Ozark Folk Speech,* Vance Randolph mentions: "One thing that impresses casual 'furriners' is the hillman's confusion in the tense forms of the verbs." As an example he mentions the use of "clumb" as the preterite for "climbed." Arkansans even laugh at themselves about these mis-pronunciations. A person who wants to show how far back in the hills he came from will say: "We was so backwards out there, we even said 'clemb' for 'clumb'"

The use of old English forms in the Ozarks has been carefully studied and documented, and shows up in phrases such as "I ain't feelin' so peert (pert)"; "I didn't mind (intend) to do that"; and "I can't tote (carry) that." One man told me that he suffered a lot of teasing in the Army before he stopped calling a sack a "poke." But neither Chaucer nor Shakespeare would have teased him, since they both used the same word with the same meaning. They also would have had no trouble understanding "skeerd" for "scared," "et" for "ate," "kivver" for "cover," or "jine" for "join."

SUPERSTITIONS AND BELIEFS

Throughout the world the horseshoe placed over an entrance is a symbol of good luck. It hangs above the doors of many Arkansas homes and barns, and is part of an ancient custom brought over by the early settlers from England. There it was believed that St. Dunstan, the

patron saint of blacksmiths, shod the Devil's hoof and
exacted from the Devil a pledge to stay away from any
building where the horseshoe was displayed.

In addition to the charm of the horseshoe there are
many other superstitions that Arkansans have inherited
from their ancestors. Most people know that it is bad luck
to put a hat on a bed; that "if your nose itches someone's
comin' with a hole in his britches"; and that a cricket on the
hearth brings good luck (another old English belief). But
here are some of the less common ones:

Lonzo Tallent reported that "If you had stale water up
there in a stream and it run over seven stones it'd be pure."
(A good thing to know in these days of pollution.)

Russell McDonough told how there were five oak trees
in front of the house where he grew up and they were all
hit by lightning at different times. He said the old
superstition was that if lightning struck more than one
time in the same place it meant that gold was buried there.

Mr. Kilgore said his wife fished in the signs to bring her
good luck, but she said no—she only fished "when the
barometer was rising." Many people spit on their fish bait
before they use it. This is probably an old superstition,
since Kevin Danaher explains, "In many parts of the world
it is considered a good and lucky thing to spit on an object
or even a person to bring good fortune or ward off evil."

Farmer Wilhite had a twinkle in his eye as he said, "*This
is a proven fact.* If you start somewhere and leave the house
and happen to think of something that you've forgotten
and you have to go back to the house—now, to keep from
having bad luck—you *make a cross mark in the road and spit
on it.* Then you can go back to the house and go on
wherever you're set—without any trouble a-tall."

Many other superstitions had to do with fire, food, and
getting married—all considered necessities in the old days!
Mr. F. Q. Browne explained that in the days before people
had matches they usually kept a small fire going and "if it
went out they would take a vessel filled with ashes and go

to a neighbor's to get coals of fire." From this practice came the expression "Come to borrow fire," which Roy Simpson explained came to mean, "I'm in a hurry—can't stay to visit." Because "borrowing fire" was so much trouble there arose several superstitions concerning the bad things that would happen if the fire went out. In discussing his parents, Fred High said, "The great trouble with them was not to let the fire go out in the spring till all the corn was planted" or they believed they would have to buy corn before another year. He said they always warned the children not to cover the fire up with cold ashes or it would go out.

There were all kinds of superstitions concerning food. Remembering the time when he developed malaria, Roy Simpson said, "I was to shake for some time before I finally conquered the disease. Many people thought I had eaten too many muscadines or small watermelons. One of my sisters-in-law believed I bathed too frequently." For years people believed that it was sinful to eat a tomato (love apple) or an onion; it was dangerous to have fish and sweet milk at the same meal; whiskey and watermelon together would kill you; and there was a "chill in every cucumber." Anyone who spilled salt was sure to have bad luck unless he threw some salt over his left shoulder to break the charm, or went to the stove and burned some salt, or spit on it. This very common superstition has been traced to the notion that Judas overturned a saltcellar during the Last Supper.

There was a belief that any girl who took the last piece of cake or bread off a plate would never get married. The same thing was true of a girl who let anyone sweep under her feet; or of the girl who fell as she went up the stairs; or the one who sat on the table. Maybe these were to warn a girl not to be greedy, lazy, or clumsy if she wanted to get a man. And certainly she should get the message in this proverb:

> A whistling girl and a crowing hen—
> Always come to a very bad end.

If she followed all these instructions carefully she could find out who her husband was to be through the old practice of naming the four corners of the room with four boys' names before she went to sleep. When she woke up the next morning the first corner she saw would be the boy she would marry. Or as Roy Simpson said, "Put a wishbone over the door and the first man through is your husband."

All "beliefs" do not have to be traditional. In a more modern vein there are many people who refuse to believe that the astronauts ever really landed on the moon. As Newman said, one of the barbers at Danville explained to him: "They're just makin' them pictures out there in Arizona." And Uncle Aaron Stevens had another logical explanation for his belief that the space program was all a bunch of foolishness.

> And they talk about goin' to the moon! Hain't no more been to the moon than I have. It takes 'em a week to fly up there, they claim; and that old moon makes a revolution round the whole outfit every twenty-four hours. If they 'us to ever get there that old moon'd pass 'em just like a car passed you goin' two hundred miles an hour and you 'us standin' in the road.

Now they claim they're gonna go to the sun. Whatta ya
know about that? Do you believe they can do it?

When I said, "They'd get kinda warm—about like it was
yesterday" (when it was 103°), Uncle Aaron's eyes lit up
because I had fallen right into his trick. He slapped his leg
and started laughing as he explained, "No! They're gonna
go in there at night."

Believing in the astronauts is just one more step in man's
struggle to understand the universe. Cephas Washburn
illustrated a similar problem among the Indians in 1820:

About this time the Mission was in receipt of supplies
from Boston. Ta-kah-to-kuh was present when these
supplies were opened. Among them was a pair of globes.
These had been taken off their frames for the convenience
of packing, wrapped in soft paper, and placed in the box.
As they were taken from the box, and divested of the
wrapping, they were laid on the counter. I observed that
they attracted the old man's attention: but true to the
characteristics of his race, he manifested no curiosity. After
a few minutes with apparent indifference, he approached
and laid his hands upon them. He then carelessly inquired
what kind of *birds* laid those eggs? I answered they were not
eggs, and told him of what and how they were made; and
placed the terrestrial globe in its frame, and showed him
how it represented the earth and its motions. "Ha!" he
replied, "what is that you say; that the earth moves?"

I told him; and illustrated it on the globe that the earth
turns on its axis every twenty-four hours. "That's a lie,"
says he; "for if the earth should turn over, all the water
would spill out, and all the rocks would fall off." This I also
endeavoured to explain. After a few minutes of deep
thought, he sent a young man, who was with him, to the
spring for a bucket of water. This he took by the bail and
swung it rapidly around. The water did not spill out,
"Oo-kuh-squah-tuh (my own name in Cherokee) is right,"
said he. "The earth turns over every day; and it is this
which causes the rising and setting sun. This subject has

always troubled me. When I was a child, I was told that the sun went back to the east in the night when we could not see it, and was ready to rise in the morning. This I knew could not be true; because the sun afforded us light, and was the cause of day. When my people have inquired of me, I have told them that there must be a hole in the foundation of the earth through which the sun passed, and so got back to the east. But this never satisfied my own mind; for I knew the sun must be immensely large, and a hole of such magnitude must weaken the foundation of the earth so much, that it could not support the earth. But now I am satisfied.

This "windmill" does more than just tell the direction of the wind. According to its owner, the vibration of the vane makes the fencepost shake and that keeps the moles out of the field.

This simple vane belongs to Uncle Sam Hess.

One very traditional group of beliefs concerns weather signs and moon lore. Rain, or the lack of it, has been of utmost importance to the farmer since agriculture began. Country people believe that animals and plants make the best weather forecasters. The hoot of the owl means a change in the weather; the crow of the cock, the howl of the wolves before sunset, or the failure of spiders to spin their webs outside foretells rain; the yawn of a cat means sunshine ahead; and the size of a goose bone or the thickness of the cornshucks determine whether it will be a mild or severe winter.

There are other common weather beliefs. If there is a ring around the moon it will soon rain, and you can tell exactly how soon by counting the number of stars in the ring. There is a star for each day until it rains. If it rains while the sun is still shining it means the Devil is beating his wife. And there are names for the unseasonable weather we sometimes have in the spring and the fall: blackberry (or dogwood) winter for a late cold snap that comes after the blackberries (or dogwood) are in bloom in the spring; and Indian summer for a late hot spell in the fall.

Many old sayings sound authoritative whether they are true or not. These include this one:

> Sow turnip seeds on the 23rd of July
> And you'll have turnips wet or dry.

And this one:

> Rain before seven,
> Shine before 'leven.

But probably the most realistic one is the old saying quoted by Fred High: "All signs fail in dry weather and all signs hit in wet."

In addition to weather beliefs there is a whole realm of moon lore that many people follow when planting their crops, riving their shingles, butchering their hogs, castrating their animals, plucking their geese, and making their soap.

Dedrick Satterfield told about his mother making lye soap: "She'd fill the ash hopper up with ashes that winter and long about March—at a certain time now in March—on a moon—well, then she'd start runnin' this lye down fixin' to make soap." One woman in Stone County said, "You always make soap and jelly on a new moon and they'll set better," and some women believe that the geese have to have their feathers picked for a feather bed only on a new moon.

Planting was (and is) done by the moon. As an old English saying warns,

> Sow peasen and beans in the wane of the moon,
> Who soweth them sooner he soweth too soon.

Fred High explained that "Men here on the creek did not start to farming 'till the hickory bark began to peel . . . and that would be the first new moon in April."

Edison Kilgore elaborated even further. "Yes, we plant in the signs. You plant when the moon is new and your stuff'll grow high and tall, but you won't reap no grain. You'll get some, but not much. But if you plant when the moon is full—when it's full and on the decrease, why you'll make a good grain crop. But for vines and stalks, why, plant in the new moon."

Patience told me, "Well, when the moon is full that's the time you plant the stuff to grow on top of the ground. You plant corn and cotton, watermelons then. They grows larger." She went on to explain that on the dark of the moon you plant things that grow underground like turnips and potatoes.

Aunt Alma said:

> On the watery sign you plant. When the moon is a-growin' you plant above the ground and when it's goin' down you plant under the ground. You dig potatoes when it's a full moon—don't dig 'em when it's growin'. (To prove her point she showed me her nice dry potatoes that had been dug on a full moon, and told me about a relative who had just recently dug his potatoes on a "growin'" moon and had ended up with nothing but rotten potatoes.)
>
> See, when the moon is gettin' smaller—after it fulls—it takes it two weeks to go down and get ready to have the first quarter. Then it begins to grow for two weeks and when it's growin' that's the time to plant your beans and peas and things; and when it's goin' down—the full moon—plant your potatoes and things underneath the ground.
>
> When it's in the feet—when the moon is full—that's the time to plant so things won't grow so tall. Your vines, if you want to plant cucumbers and things, they won't grow so long. When it's in the feet that's a good time to plant

anything to get a good root system. In the fall, if you want to put out a shrub or something, if you can plant it when the signs is in the feet the roots will grow more than the top will. Whenever you plant it when the moon's a-growin' it'll put on a big top, but if it comes a storm it's not sturdy enough to stand it.

Some of the advice appeared contradictory as the language of moon lore got complicated. Further, Granny Riddle said you should plant your beans and corn when the signs are in the arms "that's the twins." You'll get more beans on the vine and two ears of corn (instead of one) on each stalk. However she said you should not plant when the signs were in the chest or heart, and *never* plant when they were in the stomach because "the stomach throws off everything." Potatoes and peanuts should be planted in the dark of the moon "when it's in the feet," never on a new moon. After all this she added, "I don't practice this—I just preach it."

Which brings us to the question: "Does planting in the signs work?" As Edison Kilgore said, "I never have starved to death yet." Most people will assure you that "All the almanacs and all the planting guides and everything else will tell you to do that. Even the Bible'll tell you." But not all old-timers believe this. Mr. Kilgore, who is seventy-four, told about a man much older than he is, who stopped him at the store one day and asked, "Edison, do you still plant in the moon?" When Mr. Kilgore assured him that he did the old man started laughing and said, "Not me. I plant in the ground."

Almost everyone agreed that you have to kill hogs on a moon. Here are some of their explanations. Mr. Kilgore said, "I kill hogs on a full moón. The reason why—now, you kill a hog on a new moon, when the moon is on the increase, and your meat'll swell up and you won't get no grease out of it. And you kill on the full moon when it's on the decrease and your meat just tastes better, and the grease fries out of it and it don't swell up none."

Paty told what happens if you ignore the signs. "One time me and my husband killed hogs and we never thought nothing about when the moon was, but whenever we went to fryin' meat it just all went to grease. And he said to me, 'What day of the moon did we kill our hog?' and I told him. He went and looked and it was in the sign whenever you was s'posed to get more grease out of it. . . . My brother-in-law, down there, used to, he wouldn't kill a hog hardly without killin' it in the signs that way."

In a different location and a different culture Patience gave a similar explanation of the results of killing in the signs. "On the waste of the moon, that's the time you kill hogs. After the moon's full and it go to quartering then we killed hogs. But if you kill on the new moon you wouldn't get much lard—the meat would puff up. You kill on the waste of the moon so you get plenty of lard. That's the way we always done."

Hunting and Wild Animal Tales

"Stranger," said he, "in b'ar hunts I am numerous, and which particular one, as you say, I shall tell, puzzles me. There was the old she devil I shot at the Hurricane last fall—then there was the old hog thief I popped over at the Bloody Crossing, and then—Yes, I have it! I will give you an idea of a hunt, in which the greatest b'ar was killed that ever lived, none excepted: about an old fellow that I hunted, more or less, for two or three years; and if that ain't a particular b'ar hunt, I ain't got one to tell."

(T. B. Thorpe, *The Big Bear of Arkansas*)

Whether they are tall tales or so-tales, the stories that people tell about hunting and wild animals are always entertaining. Almost every man had his favorite story and each story had a wealth of folk history in it, with descriptions of house-raisings, turkey calling, rafting on the river, and a collection of frontier characters.

On a hot summer day, sitting on his front porch, Uncle Aaron Stevens promised, "I'll tell ya a bear-huntin' story." As he began telling his story he pointed to the mountains in front of us where he had hunted bears in his younger days (and where his Daddy had moved before the Civil War). The area was so remote and Uncle Aaron got so excited telling the tales that I believed them even though he had warned me, "I'll tell ya so many stories ya won't believe none of 'em." Here is what he told me:

> My daddy and my uncle, his brother [also named Aaron], was tradin' a bear on Buffalo River, and they traded him up in a cave. And they'd neither one ever went in a cave on a bear and so's they didn't know hardly what to do.

> And old Uncle Andrew Rhodes, he was a bear hunter. There was a big snow on the ground, and while they 'us there talkin' they heerd his dogs a-comin'. And they looked and seen a bear across the holler and the dogs come right on after 'im, cause he [the bear] 'us a-gettin' tard. And right at the head a the holler he clumb a tree, the bear did. The dogs treed 'im.

> Uncle Aaron says, "Now, John," says, "you never have killed a bear. You go over there and kill that un if you want to for Uncle Andrew." They knowed it was his dogs. Well, Daddy, he went over there and shot the bear out and killed him.

> Directly, here come old Uncle Andrew Rhodes on his horse in the snow after his dogs. He come up and my daddy said, "Well, I killed your bear."

> He said, "That's OK, John." He said, "That's what I'd a done when I got here." He says, "That's all right."

Uncle Aaron Stevens tells one of his hunting tales.

And my daddy says, "Well, Uncle Andrew," says, "we've
got a big 'un with big tracks trapped in a hole there, and
we've never neither one ever went in on a bear."

He says, "How much'll you give *me* to git 'im out?"

And my daddy says, "What do you want?"

He says, "I'll git 'im out for half of it."

My daddy says, "That's all right with me," so he went
over there and Uncle Aaron said, "Yeah, we'll give him half
of it."

So he [Uncle Andrew] tied a rope around both of his legs
and he went crawlin' in the hole. And he had a light that
he'd cut a chunk of fat meat outta the other bear and lit the
fire. And after while he got down so fer and he shined his
light, and that old bear he just raised up and hit his light
and knocked it down.

He says, "Bring me out, boys." And they went to pullin'
'im out as fast as they could. "Oh," he says, "there's danger
in there. All the danger there is. The hole ain't big enough
fer me and the bear both, and if he got stampeded he'd
come out and mash me to death."

He fixed 'im another light and got down there—he
knowed about where he was—and held his light so high the
bear couldn't reach him. He walked down in there and
peeped back over this bluff. [There was the bear] sittin'
back up there in a wide little crevice. And he shot
him—shot the bear! Said he was sittin' there all hunched
up. Shot him; and when the gun fired, he said, "Bring me
out, boys."

They brought him out again just as fast as they could.
"Boys," he said, "there's danger now if I hain't killed him."
They kept listenin' and listenin' and heerd 'im a-strugglin',
and after awhile he quit; and Uncle Andrew said, "I guess
he's dead."

He crawled back down in there. The bluff's about four
foot high and the bear 'us so big he couldn't lift 'im up over
this ledge. They went down there and helped him and he
said, "You'uns crawl out and pull." And he fastened that
rope around the bear's neck and said, "You'uns pull and
I'll lift." And says, "We'll get 'im outta here."

So they finally drug 'im out and Pap says there 'us blood
oozin' outta Uncle Andrew's britches legs where he'd

skinned himself on them rocks—them pullin' him out so
fast twice. But they got the bear!

I asked him what they did with the bear when they got it
home and he told how they used to hang the bear meat up
and dry it and then barbecue it. Other people smoked
their bears just like hogs. Uncle Sam Hess said about his
smokehouse, "There's been many a bear smoked in that
house."
Another one of Uncle Aaron's stories went like this:

> Old Uncle Jess Goodman used to live right over here at
> Timbo. He shot a bear way back years ago. Crippled it.
> And he was standin' there close to a cave and this bear
> made for the cave—to get in there ya know. It 'us crippled,
> it couldn't get along good. And he grabbed it by the hind
> leg and held it. And his brother come plumb across the
> holler there and shot it and killed it.
> He said it tried to bite 'im and he got up to a big tree with
> it and ever time it'd try to come around it he'd just keep
> goin' around the tree holdin' the hind leg. He was wantin' a
> bar pretty bad!
> He 'us a big man, weighed over 200 pounds, and he just
> grabbed that bear by the hind leg. And his brother, he
> come plumb across the holler and killed it.

As Uncle Aaron said when he got through telling that
story, "He was braver'n I am or had less sense one." It is
reminiscent of a story told by Aunt Ollie Gilbert. Once
there was a man who lived on the edge of the woods. One
day the preacher came by and the man asked him where
he was going. The preacher said he was going bear
hunting and asked the man to come with him. When he
hesitated, the preacher said, in his most pious voice, "Don't
be afraid—the Lord will be with us." They were deep in
the woods when along came a huge bear on his hind legs.
The man grabbed the bear by the hind leg and he and the
bear went round and around the tree. Every time the man
yelled for help the preacher called back, "Don't worry—

*Alonzo Tallent demonstrates his
cherry leaf turkey call.*

the Lord will be with you." Finally the man let go; the bear
ran off; and the man asked the preacher what on earth
happened to the Lord. To which the preacher replied,
"Oh, the Lord was with you all right. He just ain't worth a
damn in a bear fight!"

At another remote spot, Alonzo Tallent stood in his
front yard near Meyer's Creek and pointed to the
mountain where he hunted turkeys. To demonstrate his
"turkey call" he picked a cherry leaf, wet his lips, put the
edge of the leaf to his mouth, and whistled on it. As he did
this, he exclaimed, "Some people make a big curiosity out
of this; but we've done it all our lives." Then he went on to
tell about the time he got two turkeys, using a leaf to mock
them on.

I heard this turkey gobblin' and I was about a quarter of a mile from my gun. I had to go back to get my gun and when I got back over to this same place I found some leaves that I could mock a turkey on. Well, I hadn't found any turkeys the whole spring before. And when I called I got two gobblers on the mountain over that away; and I got my gun and got back over there. I got another leaf and when I called they both answered, and I got another one back over that away.

Recently, while watching a special on NET, we saw a Stone Age Indian tribe in Brazil that hunted fowl by mocking them on leaves, so this must be a very old practice.

Tom Patrick, age ninety-two, broke up laughing as he recalled this little story. "My half-brother went a squirrel huntin'. And that boy of his'n—ever time my brother'd shoot his boy'd lay down flat of his belly; you know—on the ground. So one day he laid down and stopped his years up, you know. And he'd laid down on a yeller jacket's nest! Boy, he got outta there runnin' nonstop." Possum hunting was also a popular sport and I asked what on earth they did with a possum when it was caught. Tom said, "We put it in the pot and biled it; and then put it on and baked it." Aunt Chat said they'd catch possums and skin 'em and "maybe they'd get a nickel or a dime for the skins—and that mounted to somethin'."

H. D. Payne, the same man who paid ten dollars at the box supper to eat with the woman with seven kids, told of an equally disastrous deer-hunting trip. He took his Winchester and went deer hunting one moonlit night in a farmer's vineyard. He said, "I could hear something stompin' around out there and see its eyes shining. . . . I took dead aim to be sure I wouldn't miss. When I shot I hit the farmer's mule colt right between the eyes."

Deer hunting did not usually end that way, though, since it was one of the most well-organized of the frontier sports. As Farmer Wilhite recalled: "Deer hunting was one of the main sources of wild meat through there

[Montgomery County]. The fellow that kills the deer, he gets the hide and the horns, if any; and then after the hunt is over, why then the meat is divided up among all those that are along."

Talking about his dad's good gun, he said: "It was a Sharps rifle that they used in the buffalo hunting. And my dad—as far as he could see a deer, why he could bring it down with that gun. They said that gun would shoot so far till they had to salt the bullets or else the deer would be spoilt by the time they got to it." Since deer hunting was a wintertime sport, he explained: "To hunt in the snow or sleet they'd wrap your feet in toesacks to keep your feet from skidding. Nobody had any overshoes a-tall."

The wild animal was not always hunted—sometimes it became the aggressor. Farmer went on to tell some stories about two miraculous characters, Aunt Nancy Vines and Uncle Jackson Wilhite, who both survived some unbelievable encounters with wild animals. Here are the tales:

> Well now, Grandpap and Aunt Nancy Vines, when they were married they moved first with her parents. There was lots of homestead land and Grandpap took up a homestead right adjoining Aunt Nancy's parents. He had got out logs to build a log house and they'd had the house-raising. They had the walls raised up to the plateline. The roof wasn't on then.
>
> Well, it was one day in summertime—the blackberries was ripe. And old Grandpap had taken the broadax and was down there hewing down the walls. Now it was always a funny thing to me, they go off and leave the wife without a gun a-tall—even take the dogs. Course few families had more than one gun, and when the husband was off someplace he had the gun and the dogs with him. They never thought anything about it.
>
> Aunt Nancy, she was gonna go down where her husband was a-workin'. And she passed a blackberry patch, and they was ripe and she had on her apron. You wore your apron to church or anywhere down there—it was protection for

your dress. Well, the blackberries was ripe so she gathered up her apron and she went to pickin' blackberries in her apron—gonna make a pie. And she was a-pickin' around there and she heard a racket over close to her, and she looked over there and there was a black bear—'bout the size of a calf. And so boy she lit out. She hit the trail.

Well. this bear he come down the trail behind her—just like a tame dog. And she saw that bear follerin' her. Well, she'd always heard that if a bear got after you and you had anything to eat—put a little of it down in the trail and then you light out again. Well, she put down a handful of berries and then she lit out again, and the bear come on up and gobbled up all this handful of berries and then here he starts again headin' down behind her.

Well, of course she'd been screaming bloody murder all this time. She got down to the house and Grandpap was gone! The dog had treed a squirrel off down there and so he'd took his gun and left and went down there to shoot the squirrel so they'd have some meat on the table—and him and the dog was both gone.

Well, she got there, though, and she just climbed up over the wall and got inside. She thought she'd be over in there outta the way of the bear. There she was inside this house and here the bear come climbing up that wall. Well, she'd been feedin' him, so he was gonna climb over and get in there with her. Here he come climbin' up that wall—and stickin' his feet through these cracks. Well, the broadax was layin' there and, by George, she just grabbed up that ax and as he stuck his feet through there why she just chopped one of his feet off. Well that discouraged that bear right simple. And he jumped down from the side there and she was still a-squallin' and Grandpap, he heard her yellin', and he got up there; and there was blood ever step the bear had made. So they followed it and shot the bear, and there was meat on the table—lots of it!

That was not Aunt Nancy's only encounter with a wild animal. Even after the house was built her adventures continued:

Grandpap and Aunt Nancy, they got their water at a spring down below the house there a little bit. They had the washpots and everything down by the spring so that all they'd have to carry up to the house was just the water they used there in the house.

Aunt Nancy was down there washing one day and had her baby laying on a pallet there where she was a-washin'. And so she heard this racket out to one side and she looked out there and it was a panther. And boy she quit her washin' right then and she gathered up that baby and up to the house they went.

Well, they never had made any door—they just fastened up that doorhole with a blanket that was fastened on one side—and on the other side they had some auger holes and they'd have a peg, you see, and they'd put that blanket there and stick a peg in to hold it in place. Well, she got up there and they had joists across the top and they had put some planks up there so's to store things in the loft. So the first thing, she got up on the table—table was sittin' in the middle of the floor—and she put the baby up on these boards.

And the hatchet was the only thing she could find around there—she'd left the ax down at the wash place. She got that hatchet—that was the only thing she had to fight with. She had fastened the blanket there by the door to make it as safe as she could, but she'd always heard that if a panther come around, that's supposin' you had a door, that a panther had been known to climb down the chimney. Well, they had kindlin' there handy—see, they cooked on this fireplace and had some coals left there. So she kindled up a small fire there so's to discourage him from comin' down the chimney.

Well, he got around there by this door and he was sniffin' around that and she got over there with this hatchet. He started to stick his head in between that blanket there to squeeze in and when he did he just hadn't oughta done it. Cause she whacked him in the head as hard as she could with that hatchet—and she killed 'im. And boy, she killed that panther right there!

The quick thinking of Aunt Nancy Vines was matched by the courage of Uncle Jackson Wilhite, who sounds almost too brave to be true. But this is the way Farmer told it:

> Now I had a grand-uncle, he was a brother to my grandfather; and they were moving now from Tennessee to Arkansas. And they had a flatboat. There was two or three families that came down. You see, they had freighted now from up on the Tennessee River, and they would build a flatboat and two or three families would get together and they'd put their corn and barrels of molasses and maybe a barrel of liquor, and bacon, cotton, anything they had to sell—why, they'd put that on this flatboat. And they'd go down the river. Course they'd stop at different towns and try to sell the stuff.
>
> And they just kept a-goin' until they would sell all their produce that they had raised up there in Tennessee. And so they would camp on the bank of the river at night—they would find a likely place to tie up. They had long poles that they could pole the boat if they was in a shallow place—they kept along the edges where it was shallow. And then they had what they called sweeps that was like long oars, that they could row it, you see, through deep water.
>
> Well, one night they was in the Mississippi River bottom and they'd camped there and they had a big campfire—both for heat and light, and to cook on. And there was a small girl in one of the families. And the kids had got out around the edges a little too far. And a panther jumped on this little girl. And Uncle Jackson, he was just a young man then about seventeen or eighteen years old—he jumped and he grabbed that panther by the tail to jerk it away from that girl. And they were not too far from the fire and he jumped over this campfire and dragged the panther through that fire. And when they got over there he jumped back across the fire. By that time a feller had got an ax and he chopped that panther in the head and killed it. Of course it had done scorched up the hair 'till the hide wouldn't be much good.

After Uncle Jackson married, he and Aunt Phoebe had
built a cabin. Back in those days homespun was the main
kind of tough clothing that they had. And Aunt Phoebe
had just finished making Uncle Jackson a suit of clothes
and he had put it on to see how it fit.

Every house had a fireplace—and they had a goose that
was settin' in the chimney corner there by the house. And
this goose was a-raisin' Cain out there. Well, Uncle Jackson
he run outside to see what was messin' with this goose. And
he saw what he thought was a dog there—and this goose
was a-fightin' it. Well, he just jumped off the end of the
porch and he just belted that what he thought was a dog
and he kicked it in the side.

Well, it turned on him and it turned out to be a panther.
He hollered out for Aunt Phoebe to shut and fasten the
door. And that panther jumped on him. Well, he got one
arm around it and, oh, he was a very strong fellow—said to
be one of the strongest men in that part of the country.
And with one arm he squeezed that panther to him; and it,
of course, had its mouth open a-bitin' at him. Well, he got
one hand in its mouth. He just poked his hand in its mouth
and got it by the tongue and he'd just keep inching his fist
down that panther's throat and he choked it to death. See,
he cut off its breath. And this panther was just a-clawin'
him, and it tore that brand-new suit all to pieces. It was just
in ribbons. But if he hadn't a had on a brand-new suit, why
no tellin' what it woulda done with him.

POSTSCRIPT—A WORD OF CAUTION

Now, these wild animal stories and hunting tales should
not be taken too literally. Don't be like the Apple boys
(remember the ones who asked a million questions) and
try to get the details straight on everything. One time
Bunch Clark was telling one of the Apple boys about his
experiences with a bear. Bunch had been out bird hunting
when a bear got after him and began chasing him around
a big boulder. After they had made several circles around

the rock Bunch realized there was a crack through the center of the rock and he could cut through there to make his getaway. But when he took this shortcut and came out on the other side there was the bear waiting for him. When Bunch got through telling this exciting story, the Apple boy stood there for a long, long time. Finally he asked "Was it a he bear or a she bear, Bunch?"

All of these stories that I have included were told as the absolute truth. But Farmer said later, when he was discussing the tales about Aunt Nancy Vines, that at the time the events occurred the people in the story were young and of course weren't known as "Grandpap" or "Aunt" (terms reserved for older people—regardless of their kinship to the speaker). These stories were handed down in the community and by the time they were told to Farmer these people had grown old and *he* knew them as Grandpap and Aunt Nancy, and referred to them that way in telling the story. Also a lot of "factual-sounding" details have obviously been added along the way.

In a book entitled *The Family Saga*,* the well-known Texas folklorist, Mody Boatright, discusses "The Family Saga as a Form of Folklore," and it is interesting to see how the same themes occur in various family tales. At the beginning he identifies the family saga: "I use the term mainly to denote a lore that tends to cluster around families, or often the patriarchs or matriarchs of families, which is believed to be true." That definition fits these tales precisely.

He goes on to say that the saga of a pioneer family will usually include adventures with wild animals and that, "For a story placing a human being in jeopardy, the panther was the favored animal." One of the favorite tricks in these stories is for the person who is being chased to drop food in his path to cause the animal to stop along

---

*The Family Saga and other Phases of American Folklore, Mody C. Boatright, Robert B. Downs, and John T. Flanagan. University of Illinois Press.

the way. He uses the example of a man who had killed several turkeys and dropped these one at a time in his path; just as Aunt Nancy dropped the blackberries. Also, the narrator will often tell the tale on himself (if his age, etc., makes it plausible), or on someone else he knows; for "the very art of narration encourages attribution to persons the narrator knows or knows about." Some told the stories on themselves, while Uncle Aaron told about his father and uncle, Tom Patrick chose a relative, and Farmer related tales about his friend, Aunt Nancy, and his own Uncle Jackson. Whether the stories are true or not, one thing *is* for sure—telling tall tales is an old Arkansas tradition.

Sometimes there is proof! These fish heads hung on a barn by the Buffalo River prove this fisherman's tales.

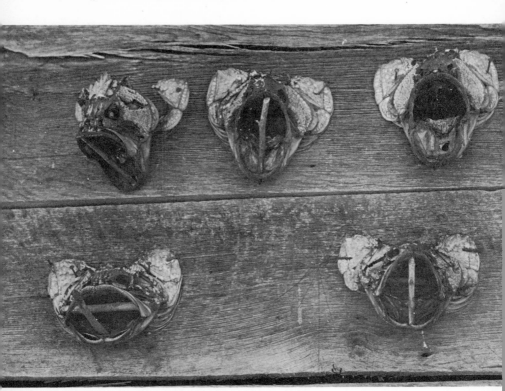

CHAPTER 8
A CALENDAR OF
FOLK EVENTS

For those who are interested in folklife, Arkansas is truly "A land for all seasons." During each time of the year there are folk events, large and small, that represent the traditional calendar customs of the area. Below is a list of these customs divided into the four seasons. For each season I have chosen some of the more interesting holidays or occasions and described them as they were yesterday and as they are today.

SPRING

Throughout the spring months there are annual festivals all over the state. Hot Springs has an outdoor art show the middle of April, Melbourne has a Pioneer Day in early May, Perryville has the Perry County Arts and Crafts Show near the end of May, and War Eagle has its "Back In the Hills" Antique Show in early May. In addition there are numerous "produce" festivals during the spring and early summer. These include a poultry festival at Batesville, a strawberry festival at Marshall, a peach

festival at Clarksville, and a pink tomato festival at
Warren.

One of the best-known folk festivals in the country is
held at Mountain View during the middle of April each
year. The festival began in a shelter cave near Blanchard
Springs in 1941, with contests for old fiddlers, cow callers,
hog callers, and jig dancers. A few months later Pearl
Harbor was attacked and the festival ended for many
years. When it started again it was held in the high school
gymnasium, where it remained until 1973, when a
multimillion-dollar folk culture center was opened at
Mountain View. Today. the show features music by the
Rackensack Society (named after an old term for
Arkansas) and crafts by the members of the Ozark Crafts
Guild; as well as songs by Jimmy Driftwood, who has been
the star of the festival since its beginning.

In an entirely different atmosphere, and with little or no
publicity, there will be authentic folk events going on all
over the state during the spring and summer months.
These are the "Decoration Days" held at the country
cemeteries for the purpose of cleaning and weeding the
cemeteries and decorating the graves. Each church has its
own traditional Sunday when its Decoration Day is held,
and these are usually timed not to interfere with other
churches in the area.

On Saturday the people who have relatives buried in the
cemetery come out in their old clothes and clean the
graves and place flowers on them. Then, on Sunday they
come in their best clothes and spend the time visiting,
singing, having lunch, and attending a memorial service.
Since Decoration Days also serve as homecomings, Roy
Simpson pointed out that "the religious element was
frequently almost submerged in the social side." He said
that people could go to a decoration somewhere "just
about every Sunday of the summer." One woman
remembered that as kids they always got a new outfit for

Spectators at the first Mountain View Folk Festival.

Performers at the first Mountain View Folk Festival at Blanchard Springs, 1941.

Decoration Day, rather than Easter, because so many people would be returning on Decoration Day.

One of the most interesting pastimes at any country cemetery is reading the tombstones and trying to guess the stories behind them. The Quapaw Indians of Arkansas put poles around their burying places and hung all manner of things on these posts. The white man often *wrote* all manner of things on his tombstones.

For example, in the Yale Cemetery G. H. Davis wanted the world to know that Kimbrell Hill saved his life during the Civil War. On his tombstone it says, "G. H. Davis of Company K. My horse was killed and fell on me. Kimbrell Hill taken him off in Price's Rade at New Toney in 1864." On a nearby tombstone we are told about "Obed, son of A. W. and L. C. Hill, Born July 23, 1888. He and three others were murdered by a bank robber at Camp Funston, Kansas, January 11, 1918."

Sometimes just the location of the grave will tell you a lot. In the old days burying someone outside the cemetery was a real disgrace and at times you will see a tombstone purposely placed just outside the fence. At the Tomahawk Cemetery the accused horse thief, Charley Deerlake, was buried outside the fence after he was shot by a posse from Missouri; since the man who owned the land where the cemetery was located didn't want him buried inside.

Mother told about the time when her Grandma Martin was dying with the smallpox. There were no doctors available on the isolated mountain where she lived, but an old man who had just moved into the area claimed to be a doctor; and so they sent for him. He declared that Grandma didn't have smallpox and to prove his diagnosis he got right down over her face and breathed. When it turned out that she did have smallpox and the disease had been spread to the others, the people were outraged and the men went after the "doctor." But when they got there he was dead—of the smallpox. To punish him they buried him outside the fence at the Possum Trot Cemetery.

Almost every cemetery has a tombstone with this old English inscription on it:

> Remember Friends as You Pass By
> As You are Now So Once was I
> As I am Now, So you shall be
> Prepare in Life to Follow me.

This epitaph leaves itself open for all kinds of "replies" such as the one I heard many years ago in England. A guide claimed that Mark Twain saw this verse on a stone in an English graveyard and, taking a piece of chalk out of his pocket, wrote underneath:

> To follow you I'd be content
> If only I knew which way you went.

This same verse and similar replies have been reported all over the country.

And then there was "Grandpa" Buckman, who lived from 1825 to 1912. He insisted that they carve just this one line on his tombstone: "Oh-Oh-Oh-Where does the dead go?" As if to answer him, the verse on the grave next to his says:

> Weep not ma-ma and Sister for me
> I am in heaven waiting for thee.

SUMMER

Greenwood has an annual arts and crafts festival in June, and in July Batesville has its White River Water Carnival, Cummins Prison has a rodeo, and Springdale has the Rodeo of the Ozarks. Near the end of July there is an old-time chicken fry on the top of Mt. Nebo, with singing, politicians making speeches, horseshoe-pitching contests, wood-chopping contests, and country crafts (plus fried chicken).

In the old days each community usually had a picnic on the Fourth of July with someone reading the Declaration of Independence, followed by an "appropriate oration," and a barbecue or fish fry. Mother remembered that they advertised as the big attraction in Belleville—"Free Ice Water." Sometimes toasts were drunk, and in 1822 the *Arkansas Gazette* listed all of the twenty-four toasts that were drunk at one Fourth of July gathering. Number thirteen sounds very familiar: "Less style and more economy at the seat of the general government."

Often a platform was built for square dancing, and my father-in-law recalled that in his community (Bear, Arkansas) they always went out to build the platform late in the evening or early in the morning when it was cool and shady at the spot; but by midafternoon on the Fourth the platform would always·be in the blazing sun—which didn't stop the dancing. He described this event:

> The platform was big enough for four squares—I'd say maybe twenty by thirty. They took it up and would store it and put it back down the next year. They'd have their fiddle and their banjoes and we'd really have a good time. They'd always have a few fist fights.
>
> There'd be a picnic all day—and possibly two days. Most of 'em would dance up till midnight—one or two o'clock—then they'd go home and rest awhile and come back the next day around ten o'clock, or noon, and they'd go up till two or three o'clock the next night.
>
> They always had a barbecue—they'd barbecue a couple of cows, you know, for the picnic—they dug pits in the ground. Usually the politicians would be there and make speeches.

Gerstaeker described an even earlier celebration in Arkansas:

The Fourth of July came. I walked four miles to the place where the barbecue was to be given. When I got there, it seemed as if everybody from miles around was present. The assembled crowd, typical of farms and woods, made a colorful picture. Some wore hunting shirts, some were dressed in homespun, woolen coats, others putting comfort before fashion stood around with sleeves rolled up. Over an outdoor fire huge roasts were steaming; in a shady place near the house women were brewing huge quantities of coffee.

Even before I reached the house I could hear the wailing of music of a single fiddle. In one wing of the double-house the young people were dancing. Not familiar with the gay and rather strenuous dances of the people here, I amused myself by observing the colorful groups that had come in from all corners of the county . . . .

When noon came, a long table was set in front of the house, and chairs and benches were placed along-side. Since it was impossible to seat everyone at the first table, the women ate first—contrary to the home practice of the Americans. The young men served. The meal consisted of beef and pork roast, sweet potatoes, white potatoes, cornbread, cake, milk, and coffee. One man brought a keg of wine for the ladies. In a surprisingly short time they had emptied it. After the dinner was finished, a man made a speech in honor of the Fourth of July. Then the dances started again. I was interested to observe different groups, entertaining themselves in various ways, which were gathered picturesquely around the house. One party of strong, sunburned hunters lay on the grass boasting of their experiences. I noticed that two men were sitting on the trunk of a fallen tree playing cards. Elsewhere others were engaged in a broad-jumping contest, making truly astonishing jumps by swinging a heavy stone in each hand and throwing it behind at the instant of the leap. Several tall fellows were asleep in the shade of a tree.

All of this merrymaking was not without its conse-
quences. Aunt Alma recalled one of the saddest days of
her life—the Sunday after the Fourth of July when she was
about seven years old. That morning she hid her face
behind her mother's long skirts as they stood in the back of
the church while her father was called up to the front and
turned out of the church for square dancing at the Fourth
of July picnic.

In August there is an event that is almost dying out—the
Old Soldiers' Reunion—held at Heber Springs every
summer since shortly after the Civil War. When Brandy
Baswell was a little boy he began attending them with his
father, and in 1972 he attended his eighty-fifth reunion.
He describes a reunion as it was in the old days:

> There would be thousands of 'em, blue and gray,
> Confederates and Yankees, too. They had their old
> uniforms and they would march six abreast—they would
> be two or three miles long back this way, see? Drums and
> everything—and they'd march down Main Street.
>
> They had big long pits to barbecue the meat—the
> farmers would furnish the meat free, you see. It'd be three
> days, this reunion would be. The merchants furnished the
> bread and everything was free—nobody paid for anything.
>
> And they'd tell stories about the old times and they was
> all friends, you know, the Yankees and Confederates. They
> would have these barbecue pits. They'd barbecue every
> kind of meat you could think of—lambs, beef, pork,
> chickens—all free. A lot of the ladies would bake some
> bread themselves and bring it. They came from every-
> where and would camp here for three days. We had a
> reunion the other day but it's just about played out. These
> young ones, you know, they don't put much in it.

Both the Fourth of July picnic and the Old Soldiers
usually had a jenny-ride. "Jennie" is a gypsy word
meaning merry-go-round and that is about what a
jenny-ride was. It was the only thing the soldiers had to

pay for at their reunion, and Brandy Baswell describes it: "A feller by the name of Jeems R. Martin had a merry-go-round and a mule pulled it, you know—and you paid a nickel to ride. And it had a post driven up out here and rings on it. They'd give you a stick and as you'd go by if you could hook a ring you'd get a free ride. Ever so often they changed mules because the mule going round and round got dizzy. This was called the jenny-ride."*

AUTUMN

In the fall there are Arts and Crafts Fairs at War Eagle Mills, Eureka Springs, Pine Bluff, and Mountain Home. There is a Clothesline Fair at Prairie Grove and a Flaming Fall Revue Festival at Rogers. The "Ozark Frontier Trail Festival and Craft Show," held in Heber Springs during October, includes a sorghum mill, a water-witching demonstration, a pioneer parade, muzzle-loading rifle firing, Indian craft demonstrations, and spinning contests. They have street dancing, folklore displays in the business windows, and an antique show; as well as a "Folk Heritage Musical Program" in the park.

Up in the northern part of the state there is a little town called Altus that was settled by a few German and Swiss families in the 1880's. The first settlers planted the vineyards that have since made the area famous for its wine-making. On a Saturday afternoon in October the Altus Wine Festival is held, with German dancers, tours of the vineyards, a "grape-stomping" contest, a German dinner, and fireworks in the evening.

All over the state during the autumn months the counties are carrying on that old English tradition—the Harvest Fairs. These began in the Middle Ages as a respite from the drudgery of daily life and were held after the harvest was gathered in. In England they were usually

*"Jennie" is also a term for a mule.

held where the drove roads came together, but in
Arkansas they are held at the fairgrounds in each county
seat.

Most of these fairs have "degenerated" into midways
with rides and games of chance, but there are usually a few
booths of home-grown produce tucked away at the rear of
the fairgrounds; and some fairs still feature such old-time
events as catching greased pigs, beard-growing contests,
calf roping, etc. When we start to complain about the sorry
state of modern-day fairs we will have to admit that they
are still one of the best places to purchase home-canned
foods and handmade quilts. Also, we should realize that
our complaint is not a new one. In the early 1800's Cephas
Washburn met an old Indian who "lamented most deeply
the degeneracy of his people." He told Washburn that the
Indians had formerly held an "annual feast of First-Fruits"
in the fall after the harvest. The minister told how:

> This led to the inquiry on my part as to the intention of
> that festival, which the old man replied that formerly in all
> their towns, before eating of any of the green corn, there
> was held a solemn festival, preceded by a strict fast, taking
> some powerful purgative medicine, and a complete
> ablution of all persons and their apparel. Then some of the
> finest ears of corn were offered in thanksgiving.

According to the old Indian the only part left was the
Green Corn Dance, and even that was "utterly desecrated
by the introduction of fire-water!"

WINTER

Winter is the slow season for festivals, but there is an
annual Wild Turkey Calling Contest and Turkey Trot at
Yellville in late October and a World Championship Duck
Calling Contest at Stuttgart in December. All over the state
Christmas is ushered in with parades and pageants, and on
Lake Hamilton Santa Claus arrives on a decorated barge.

Many people today are trying to take the commercialism out of the holiday season and return Christmas to its "old ways." Here are some of the Christmas memories that older people gave me when I asked them how they celebrated the holiday when they were young.

PATIENCE—

We hung our stockings at the fireplace on Christmas Eve night. We got candy and apples and some kinda doll and little white sheeps with the wool on them—things like that. We didn't never get an apple and orange all through the year like they do now. It was a pleasure too, cause we didn't see no toys till Christmas.

We had Christmas trees. We decorated 'em with different papers and stuff like that. We'd go out in the woods and cut our Christmas tree—a holly bush. You know they used to be plentiful round here. They'd have them red balls on 'em. We'd do it a day or two 'fore Christmas. We used to string popcorn. We didn't have no cranberries—we'd get them red haws and things. Make candy—pour it on a buttered plate.

On Christmas Day the older people they went to church 'fore day in the morning—they had a 'fore-day service. They'd leave home about four o'clock in the morning and they'd go to church and stay till day. They'd come back after it was day. Out here at Pleasant Grove now they have a 'fore-day meetin' on Christmas.

When the old folks went to church—us little children, we'd be in bed. And when we'd wake up we'd get up and look at our presents.

JIM BIXLER—

They used to fire the anvil at Christmas, and also had another custom. I've seen my grandpa take an auger and bore a big hole in the tree—deep in there—and fill that full of gunpowder, and drive a peg in there and set that off on Christmas. Maybe then next spring they'd be a-plowin' and you know they'd find that peg—maybe it'd blew it nearly a quarter a mile.

Wilce Thomas was one of the people who had celebrated "Old Christmas" as a child—

> Old Christmas is twelve days from New Christmas —there's just twelve days betwixt them two dates. And when I 'us a little old boy, why I didn't know there was any other Christmas—till that New Christmas come around.
>
> Old Uncle Lewis Brandon and Aunt Bessie Brandon, they was about eighty then—that was the first time I ever heerd of New Christmas. They said, "The twenty-fifth day of December, that's what they're gonna use for Christmas now." And we've been using it ever since.

Wilce said he had never heard of a Christmas tree until they started having them at "meetin's"; and for a present he always got "a dime's worth of peppermint candy—ever year. Done that till I was a married man nearly."

Hadie Payne was another man who remembered "Old Christmas" and some of its traditions: "I think it's January sixth . . . it's been so long I can't remember. They used to tell me a story about that—said the cows'd get down on their knees, and the elderberries would turn to wine—no, the water would turn to wine. That was it. . . . Anyhow, I stayed awake one night to see if the water would turn to wine. Didn't nothin' happen."*

Sometimes Old Christmas came in handy for hard-pressed parents. As one woman recalled, "One time Santy Claus wasn't able to come to our place very much, so on Old Christmas Santy Claus came. And Mother explained to us that Santy Claus was delayed and so he came late because this was still Christmas—it was· called Old Christmas. I think it was about twelve days after Christmas."

There were some superstitions associated with the

---

*These were old English beliefs. The idea of the cattle kneeling in homage at midnight on Christmas Eve was immortalized in a poem by Thomas Hardy: "If someone said on Christmas Eve, 'Come; see the oxen kneel. . . .' I should go with him in the gloom, Hoping it might be so."

twelve days between Old and New Christmas. These days supposedly determined the prevailing weather for the twelve months of the year—the first day told you what type of weather January would have, etc. Some people felt that it was bad luck to do your washing or to buy anything new during these twelve days. For those who had doubts about the proper date, the old "Cherry Tree Carol" had Joseph asking when the baby's birthday would be, and Jesus himself replying: "On the sixth day of January my birthday will be."

When I asked people to tell me the Christmas they remembered the best, most people recalled the programs they had at school when "kids would dress up in old ragged clothes and black their faces" and the "teacher gave the children treats—such as apples or stick candy." Others remembered getting "fruit and hard candy at the church." Perhaps apples and candy don't sound like a lot to us; but in the early days, when orchards were scarce, apples were a real treat and store-bought candy was a rarity.

Aunt Willie and Aunt Edna remembered the Christmas that they almost didn't have any apples. On Christmas Eve a family from the "big mountain" had been to Dardanelle to sell their apples and were coming back home across Chickalah Mountain. In the front of their wagon they had put a branch of an apple tree to "advertise" that they were apple peddlers; and in the back of the wagon they had some baskets of unsold apples. About dusk Grandpa saw them coming down the road and hurried out to buy a basket of apples, but he didn't tell the children. That night as they sat around the fire, with Grandmother in the kitchen doing the cooking for the next day, the children started feeling sad because there weren't any apples for Christmas. Just then two or three apples came rolling across the floor toward them. They couldn't believe their eyes; and as they sat there talking about it, some more apples came rolling across the floor. It took them a little while before they realized that the apples were being rolled in there by Grandmother, who was in the kitchen working away.

Another person who remembered his "lucky" Christmas was Hadie Payne. When I asked him what he got for Christmas when he was a child, he replied, "mostly firecrackers was all ever I got." But his best Christmas came during the Depression when he had no food and no money and was riding the freight trains looking for work. "One time I got down here in a small town and it was the day before Christmas, and a whole big bunch of people had all gathered up around there. And there was a man up on top of a building—he had a turkey. He was holding a turkey up there. He says, 'Now, whoever catch the turkey he would get the turkey.' Well, I was a stranger, I didn't know nobody. Well, here come Mister Turkey and it looked like he flew right square into my arms. And I got the turkey!"

The best part of Christmas was the chance it gave families to get together for visiting and festivities. From miles around they gathered together, and Aunt Willie recalled the joy on Christmas Day when "someone looked out and saw Uncle Billy's family driving up in the hack." They exchanged gifts, ate dinner, sang some songs ("Uncle Billy sang bass, Aunt Ada tenor, and the children filled in the other parts",), and then the old folks visited while the younger ones played.

Farmer Wilhite recalled one of the old, old play-party games that they played in the log cabins of the Ouachita Mountains:

THREE LITTLE GIRLS A-SKATING

Three little girls a-skating went,
    A-skating went, a-skating went,
Three little girls a-skating went,
    All on a Christmas morning.

(See, they hold hands and go round and around and around—the three of 'em.)

The ice was thin—they all fell in,
  They all fell in, they all fell in,
The ice was thin—they all fell in,
  All on a Christmas morning.

Three little boys to help them out,
  To help them out, to help them out,
Three little boys to help them out,
  All on a Christmas morning.

(So they help 'em out. Then they play—)

Around and around and around we go,
  Around we go, around we go,
Around and around and around we go,
  All on a Christmas morning.

(Then the three little girls they get out and three little boys
stay in and they go over it again.)

Three little boys a-skating went,
  A-skating went, a-skating went,
Three little boys a-skating went,
  All on a Christmas morning.

Thank You Notes

We're coming, Arkansas,
We're coming, Arkansas.
Our four-horse team
Will soon be seen
In the hills of Arkansas.

The roads are rough down there,
And you will find it so,
Hills and hollows,
Rocks and stumps,
In the hills of Arkansas.

("We're Coming Arkansas"—as sung by Noble Cowden)

Somehow they all came to Arkansas—these people or their ancestors. They traveled in various ways. Some came in true wagon trains; while one woman's father hired two boxcars and put the family and furniture in one and the horses and cows in the other. When they got here they discovered that conditions were not always the best. One man said the place where they homesteaded was such poor land that "The saying was, 'It'd take *three* Irishmen with *two* jugs of whiskey to even raise a fuss!'" Another man told how his father came into the "sunk lands" of Arkansas and bought out an established homestead:

When he bought that he bought the clearing, the squatter's rights, the house, an old blue mule, a red cow, and fourteen goats—one billy goat and thirteen nanny goats. Two years later the high water came along; the Mississippi River flooded and water came over the whole thing. So we took some big cottonwood logs and put 'em together and made a raft to save our stock. We put the cow and the billy goat and the nanny goats up on the raft. And the billy goat butted all the nannies off and they drowned—and the cow kicked the billy goat off and *he* drowned. So I went out of the stock business.

But no matter how they traveled or what the environment was when they got here, they all developed a common trait—hospitality. This section is a special thank you to my patient family, Russ, Lee Anne, and Russell; and to all the people who came to their gates and said, "Welcome." Below I have listed their names in alphabetical order, along with the counties where they live and some of their birthdays. In the book I have referred to many of them as Aunt, Uncle, Brother, and Granny, even though they were not *all* blood kin to me. This was the way they were known in their communities and this was the way I met them.

Each person in this book was unique, but they all shared a great knowledge of Arkansas traditions. The one thing that you could safely say of all of them is an old Irish expression: "We shall not see their like again." So, "Thank you" again to these people who took the time to remember:

Myra Adams—Saline County
Ed Ballentine—Stone County, September 19, 1905
Algie Bettis—Garland Country, 1894
A. A. "Brandy" Baswell—Cleburne County, June 6, 1885
J. C. "Jim" Bixler—Garland County
Bill Blevins—Carroll County, November 7, 1892
Bob Blair—Stone County
F. Q. Browne—Grant County, 1898
Lieutenant Colonel John Buxton—Pulaski County
Annie Campbell—Pulaski County, January 7, 1887
Alma Dodd—Garland County
Roxie Dooley—Yell County, August 29, 1883
Jimmy Driftwood—Stone County
John Gideon—Piedmont, Kansas
Ollie Gilbert—Stone County, October 17, 1892
Roland Gillihan—Stone County
Sim Goodman—Grant County, December 31, 1887
Lillian and Joe Hale—Pulaski County

Mrs. Arch Hardgrave—Pulaski County, 1882
Mr. Arch Hardgrave—Pulaski County, 1877
Violet Hensley—Marion County
Sam Hess—Stone County, December 21, 1880
Lourinda Hoggard—Faulkner County, 1879
Floyd Holland—Stone County, March 9, 1891
Mrs. John Joyce—Pulaski County
Edison Kilgore—Yell County
Polly Lancaster—Garland County
Eppes Mabrey—Stone County
Russell and Violet McDonough—Garland County
Rosie McKay—Perry County
Tom McKinnon—Washington County
Athlea and Elmer Moody—Stone County
Kermit Moody—Stone County
Walter Moody—Stone County
Edna Moore—Pulaski County, October 10, 1884
Cecil Murray—Newton County
Dr. Olen Nail—Craighead County
Ila Nixon—Pulaski County
Paty Owens—Saline County
Louise Parsons—Pulaski County
Tom Patrick—Madison County, 1880
H. D. "Hadie" Payne—Pulaski County
Frances Petrovicz—Boone County
Arthur Pledger—Yell County
Jim Dan Powell—Stone County, August 6, 1883
Caroline and Andy Rainbolt—Stone County
Almeda Riddle—Cleburne County, November 21, 1898
Dedrick Satterfield—Carroll County, February 23, 1888
Roy Vergil Simpson—Washington County, August 6, 1896
Guy Smith—Garland County
Chat Lawrence Standridge—Montgomery County, October 22, 1888
Aaron Stevens—Stone County, March 10, 1884
Newman and Lillie Sugg—Yell County

Willie Sugg—Pulaski County, August 27, 1889
M. S. Sumler—Lonoke County
Alonzo Tallent—Garland County, May 20, 1889
Letta Taylor—Cleburne County
Coy Wilse Thomas—Searcy County, November 28, 1886
Faye Underwood—Logan County
Mr. and Mrs. Clyde Villines—Newton County
Essie Ward—Searcy County
Ray Whitfield—Stone County
Walter Whitfield—Stone County
Warren Farmer and Bessie Wilhite—(See Postscript)
Mr. and Mrs. Edgar Williams—Stone County
Irene Williams—Yell County
Melvina "Patience" Wilson—(See Postscript)
E. L. and Roberta Wittenberg—Pulaski County
Walter Yardley—Stone County

The pictures were taken by my husband or myself and were developed by Wayne Bolick of Little Rock. The only exceptions were the photos of the first Mountain View Folk Festival, which were provided by Mr. L. A. Kingsbury of New Franklin, Missouri.

There were many people who very graciously gave me permission to quote from various books on the subject of folklore. The authors of these books were:

Kevin Danaher, whose books on Irish folk customs make fascinating reading and an excellent basis for the discovery of Irish traditions that exist in Arkansas. His works include: *In Ireland Long Ago, Irish Country People, Gentle Places and Simple Things,* and *The Pleasant Land of Ireland,* all published by The Mercier Press, 4 Bridge Street, Cork. (By permission of the author.)

Fred High, who was born on January 15, 1878 ("I was born after midnight, so I never could sleep very good in the after part of the night") in Carroll County, Arkansas. He had privately printed three books containing family history, old folksongs, sayings, etc., that are full of Ozark history: *It Happened in the Ozarks, Forty-Three Years for Uncle Sam,* and *Old, Old Folk Songs.* (Permission to quote from these was granted by his son, Frank High.)

Mary Randolph, who wrote a book entitled *The Virginia Housewife: or Methodical Cook* that first appeared in 1824. The section entitled "To Cure Bacon" was taken from this book. (Quoted by permission of The Valentine Museum, Richmond, Virginia.)

Cephas Washburn, whose *Reminiscences of the Indians* was first published in 1869, and was republished in 1955 by Hugh Park. The book is available from The Press-Argus, Van Buren, Arkansas. (Permission was granted by Mr. Park.)

Mr. Leo Rainey, who gave permission to quote from the song, "We're Coming Arkansas," as published in his book *Songs of the Ozark Folk.*

Other sources that were helpful included: (For local history and customs)—

Pioneers and Makers of Arkansas—Josiah H. Shinn.

All of Vance Randolph's works, especially *Down in the Holler—a Gallery of Ozark Folk Speech* by Vance Randolph and George P. Wilson.

County histories, such as—

History of Ashley County by Y. W. Etheridge.

History of Lawrence, Jackson, Independence and Stone Counties, Arkansas by S. W. Stockard.

The writings of Friedrich Gerstaeker (a German traveler who made several trips to Arkansas in the early 1800's). Excerpts from his works were translated by Professor Clarence Evans and published in various issues of the *Arkansas Historical Quarterly.*

Stars Upstream by Leonard Hall.

For comparison with other folk cultures —

A complete series of books published by Shire Publications of England on English folklore, including:

English Customs and Traditions, Margaret Gascoigne.
Discovering the Folklore of Birds and Beasts, Venetia Newall.
Discovering the Folklore of Plants, Margaret Baker.
Discovering Folklore in Industry, Alan Smith.
Discovering English Fairs, Margaret Baker.
The publications of the *Southern Folklore Quarterly.*
A Treasury of Georgia Folklore by Ronald G. Killion and Charles T. Waller.

For a study of music and games—

A Singer and Her Songs, by Almeda Riddle (edited by Roger D. Abrahams). This delightful book not only tells the story of Granny's life, but also gives fifty of her authentic Arkansas folksongs together with the music.
Modern Rudiments of Music (shape notes), still published by the Stamps-Baxter Music Company.
White Spirituals in the Southern Uplands by George Pullen Jackson.
Games and Songs of American Children by William Wells Newell.
American Folk Tales and Songs by Richard Chase.
String Games for Beginners by Kathleen Haddon.

One Last Postscript—Three Unique Arkansans

Everybody who contributed to this book was a very special person. Since I can't go down the list and tell the life story of each one I would like to close with the stories of three who were each unusual in their own way.

The first of course is Warren Farmer Wilhite. He is the answer to every folklore collector's dream—a marvelous storyteller, a person who has really lived on the frontier and done the things that are now just a page in a history book for most people, and close at hand. The last-mentioned was important because it obviously took many, many taping sessions to obtain the material that he contributed to this book. He and his wife, Bessie, always welcomed me into their home and we soon became the best of friends.

Here is a little of Farmer's own personal story. On May 4, 1891, he was born in Cherokee County, Texas. His daddy had gone there from Arkansas, and shortly after the turn of the century Farmer's family left Texas, heading back toward Arkansas. There were three wagons full of family members, and as he said, "We was kind of a wrong-way Carrigan outfit—we was comin' from the West toward the East."

Their first stop was with relatives in Franklin County, Texas, and there, "It rained so much we got mudbound— and we knew we'd never get to Arkansas in time to raise a crop the next year. And so we stayed one year there in Franklin County." But Arkansas' promise of homestead land, fine timber, etc., attracted his daddy, and the next year they continued on to Arkansas. About the trip Farmer said:

> We had such a heavy load and a light team till everybody that was big enough had to walk so's to lighten the load. So my dad—he was one that walked. My older sister walked

and my mother, she rode in the wagon to take care of the
younger kids. Well, when we'd get to a town all that was
walking they'd get in the wagon so's to not be too obvious.
So except through towns, when my dad drove, why, I
drove just about every step of the way from there into
Arkansas. (He was twelve years old!)

When they arrived, his daddy had "thirty-five dollars, a
wagon, a team, a wife, and seven kids." And it took sixteen
of those thirty-five dollars to file on the homestead. They
discovered that some of the land was so poor it was almost
impossible to raise a crop. The next year they moved to
Montgomery County in the Ouachita Mountains, and that
is the source of Farmer's reminiscences. Today he lives in
Pulaski County, where he came as a young man, married
Bessie Wiggins, and raised a family of his own. In addition
to his abilities as a storyteller, he is an inventor, designer,
naturalist, and musician.

Another charming person who became a good friend
was Melvina Wilson—whom everyone rightly calls "Patience." She was born September 28, 1888, near Bearskin
Lake in Lonoke County. When Melvina was four years old
her mother died and she was raised by her grandmother.
This grandmother was born about 1808 and had grown
up as a slave in Kentucky. According to Patience she "lived
to get way over a hundred—she was a hundred and
somethin' when she died. She just died in 1913."

Her grandmother saw a lot of changes in the world, but
the one thing that Patience remembered her talking about
the most was the time the stars fell in the South. "You
heard about when the stars fell? That was way back in
slavery time. They said it got dark, so dark, that the
chickens went to roost at nine o'clock in the morning."
Patience was disappointed that I hadn't heard of this
phenomenon and assured me: "It was in all the old
histories."

Sure enough, I found it mentioned in two local histories.
In one the author told how a neighbor discussed the comet

of 1858 and, "He said it recalled to his mind the great
meteoric display in 1833, in Kentucky, which caused great
excitement among all classes, many of whom believed that
the world was coming to an end; some making hasty
preparation for the judgment day." And in an early
Arkansas history an old man said, "We saw the stars fall in
1833. We ran out and tried to catch them . . . . Lots of
people were scared and got down to pray. They thought
the world was coming to an end."*

Patience lives alone now with several dogs and cats for
company in a neat white house, not far from the spot
where she was born. Her philosophy on old age was
expressed as she told me about an article she had read on a
man who had just turned 113: "He was celebratin' it in the
wrong way. He say give him good wine, and good women,
and dancin'. Look like a feller that old oughta say, 'Give
me Jesus.'"

This marvelous woman has truly lived up to her name as
I have persistently questioned her about "old times." Not
only has she explained things to me patiently, but when I
asked her about cutting designs out of paper she got her
scissors and demonstrated, and when I asked her about
making molasses candy she got out her sorghum and
made me some. When I asked her about Fifth Sunday
services, she invited me to attend the one at her church.
No one could ask for a better friend.

The third person was someone I never met—the
Reverend Cephas Washburn. In 1818 one of the
Cherokee chiefs asked the Protestant Mission Board to
send missionaries to his homeland in the northwest part of

*People's reactions have not changed so much since then. In September, 1973, a number
of mysterious objects fell from the Southern skies and one man in Georgia declared that it
was brimstone from heaven sent down by God to show that he could burn the earth.
However, others were more blasé about it. In Alabama a piece of blue ice "about the size of a
No. 3 washtub" fell on the same date and the local officials put it in a freezer so everyone
could see it. People in Arkansas and all over the South immediately began seeing UFO's, and
another man in Georgia, who admitted that he had indulged in a couple of drinks while
watching the skies, said that he had shared a sandwich with his space visitors. Later, two men
in Mississippi went for a ride with theirs.

Arkansas. Two years later Cephas Washburn and his brother-in-law, Alfred Finney, had arrived with their families and established the Dwight Mission. The Indians offered them their choice of sites and they chose a beautiful spot in Pope County on the Salaiseau (Sallisaw) River. In the beginning they erected two cabins, but soon they were joined by other missionaries and eight years later they had built thirty buildings, including a school for the Cherokee people.

Disease plagued these early missionaries and at times life was extremely hard, but they were constantly impressed with the intelligence, sense of humor, and goodwill of the Cherokees. In addition to major problems they were often thwarted by minor problems such as their difficulty in finding interpreters in whom they had confidence. At one time Mr. Washburn began to suspect that the interpreter was adding comments of his own to the sermons, and he questioned another Indian in whose honesty he trusted. The Indian agreed that the interpreter was not faithful and gave the reverend an example where the interpreter had said:

> Washburn tells me to say to you that, in the sight of God, there are but two kinds of people, the good people and the bad people. But I do not believe him. I believe that there are three kinds; the good people, the bad people, and a middle kind, that are neither good nor bad, just like myself.

Years later Cephas Washburn published his book entitled *Reminiscences of the Indians,* telling about his life among the Cherokees. If it is true, as some people have pointed out, that in America the only truly native folklore was that of the American Indians, then American folklorists are greatly indebted to Washburn. His interest in the Indians led him to chronicle their superstitions, beliefs, and customs; and his care in recording the details of their folk life gave us one of the most valuable contributions to Arkansas folklore.

Today, most of Dwight Mission lies beneath the waters of Lake Dardanelle. An historic marker on the banks, the rock outlines of some buildings, and a few graves on a nearby hillside are all that are left of the site. Cephas Washburn is buried in Mt. Holly Cemetery in Little Rock and the memory of his great concern for the Indians lives on in his charming book of reminiscences.

INDEX